Sleep Disorders

THE STATE OF
MENTAL ILLNESS
AND ITS THERAPY

THE STATE OF
MENTAL ILLNESS
AND ITS THERAPY

Sleep Disorders

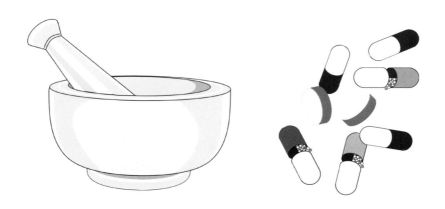

Joan Esherick

Mason Crest

Mason Crest
450 Parkway Drive, Suite D
Broomall, PA 19008
www.masoncrest.com

Printed in the Hashemite Kingdom of Jordan.

First printing
9 8 7 6 5 4 3 2 1

Series ISBN: 978-1-4222-2819-7
ISBN: 978-1-4222-2837-1
ebook ISBN: 978-1-4222-8998-3

The Library of Congress has cataloged the
hardcopy format(s) as follows:

Library of Congress Cataloging-in-Publication Data

Esherick, Joan.
[Drug therapy and sleep disorders]
Sleep disorders / Joan Esherick.
    pages cm. – (The state of mental illness and its therapy)
Audience: Age 12.
Audience: Grade 7 to 8.
Revision of: Drug therapy and sleep disorders. 2004.
Includes bibliographical references and index.
ISBN 978-1-4222-2837-1 (hardcover) – ISBN 978-1-4222-2819-7 (series) – ISBN 978-1-4222-8998-3 (ebook)
1. Sleep disorders–Juvenile literature. 2. Sleep disorders–Chemotherapy–Juvenile literature. I. Title.
RC547.E835 2014
616.8'498061–dc23
                              2013008251

Produced by Vestal Creative Services.
www.vestalcreative.com

Picture Credits:
Artville: pp. 10, 12, 14, 19, 25, 28, 30, 31, 33, 34, 38, 66, 74, 86, 90, 92, 113, 118, 119, 120; Corbis: p. 108; Image Ideas: p. 37; Image Source: pp. 71, 89, 94, 97; National Library of Medicine: pp. 49, 50; PhotoDisc: pp. 53, 54, 68, 78, 98, 111, 114; Rubberball: pp. 26, 84, 106; Stockbyte: p. 80. The individuals in these images are models, and the images are for illustrative purposes only. To the best knowledge of the publisher, all other images are in the public domain. If any image has been inadvertently uncredited or miscredited, please notify Vestal Creative Services, Vestal, New York 13850, so that rectification can be made for future printings.

CONTENTS

Introduction

by Mary Ann McDonnell

Teenagers have reason to be interested in psychiatric disorders and their treatment. Friends, family members, and even teens themselves may experience one of these disorders. Using scenarios adolescents will understand, this series explains various psychiatric disorders and the drugs that treat them.

Diagnosis and treatment of psychiatric disorders in children between six and eighteen years old are well studied and documented in the scientific journals. A paper appearing in the *Journal of the American Academy of Child and Adolescent Psychiatry* in 2010 estimated that 49.5 percent of all adolescents aged 13 to 18 were affected by at least one psychiatric disorder. Various other studies have reported similar findings. Needless to say, many children and adolescents are suffering from psychiatric disorders and are in need of treatment.

Many children have more than one psychiatric disorder, which complicates their diagnoses and treatment plans. Psychiatric disorders often occur together. For instance, a person with a sleep disorder may also be depressed; a teenager with attention-deficit/hyperactivity disorder (ADHD) may also have a substance-use disorder. In psychiatry, we call this comorbidity. Much research addressing this issue has led to improved diagnosis and treatment.

The most common child and adolescent psychiatric disorders are anxiety disorders, depressive disorders, and ADHD. Sleep disorders, sexual disorders, eating disorders, substance-abuse disorders, and psychotic disorders are also quite common. This series has volumes that address each of these disorders.

Major depressive disorders have been the most commonly diagnosed mood disorders for children and adolescents. Researchers don't agree as to how common mania and bipolar disorder are in children. Some experts believe that manic episodes in children and adolescents are underdiagnosed. Many times, a mood disturbance may co-occur with another psychiatric disorder. For instance, children with ADHD may also be depressed. ADHD is just one psychiatric disorder that is a major health concern for children, adolescents, and adults. Studies of ADHD have reported prevalence rates among children that range from two to 12 percent.

Failure to understand or seek treatment for psychiatric disorders puts children and young adults at risk of developing substance-use disorders. For example, recent research indicates that those with ADHD who were treated with medication were 85 percent less likely to develop a substance-use disorder. Results like these emphasize the importance of timely diagnosis and treatment.

Early diagnosis and treatment may prevent these children from developing further psychological problems. Books like those in this series provide important information, a vital first step toward increased awareness of psychological disorders; knowledge and understanding can shed light on even the most difficult subject. These books should never, however, be viewed as a substitute for professional consultation. Psychiatric testing and an evaluation by a licensed professional are recommended to determine the needs of the child or adolescent and to establish an appropriate treatment plan.

Foreword
by Donald Esherick

We live in a society filled with technology—from computers surfing the Internet to automobiles operating on gas and batteries. In the midst of this advanced society, diseases, illnesses, and medical conditions are treated and often cured with the administration of drugs, many of which were unknown thirty years ago. In the United States, we are fortunate to have an agency, the Food and Drug Administration (FDA), which monitors the development of new drugs and then determines whether the new drugs are safe and effective for use in human beings.

When a new drug is developed, a pharmaceutical company usually intends that drug to treat a single disease or family of diseases. The FDA reviews the company's research to determine if the drug is safe for use in the population at large and if it effectively treats the targeted illnesses. When the FDA finds that the drug is safe and effective, it approves the drug for treating that specific disease or condition. This is called the labeled indication.

During the routine use of the drug, the pharmaceutical company and physicians often observe that a drug treats other medical conditions besides what is indicated in the labeling. While the labeling will not include the treatment of the particular condition, a physician can still prescribe the drug to a patient with this disease. This is known as an unlabeled or off-label indication. This series contains information about both the labeled and off-label indications of psychiatric drugs.

I have reviewed the books in this series from the perspective of the pharmaceutical industry and the FDA, specifically focusing on the labeled indications, uses, and known side effects of these drugs. Further information can be found on the FDA's website (www.FDA.gov).

How we feel during the day depends a lot on how we slept the night before.

Chapter One

A Good Night's Sleep

How long did you sleep last night? Six hours? Maybe seven? Did you sleep long enough? You may think you did, but one February evening in 1990 a New Hampshire teenager thought he'd gotten enough sleep, too. He was wrong.

Seventeen-year-old Michael Doucette wasn't just any ordinary teenager. In 1989 the conscientious student entered and won a national driver safety competition where he earned the title, "America's Safest Teen Driver." As the first place winner, he was awarded a brand new Dodge Shadow to use for one year. Just a few months after winning the title, while driving his prize on a highway near his Concord home, Michael Doucette fell asleep. His automobile crossed the center line and collided head on with an oncoming vehicle. Both "America's Safest Teen Driver" and the 19-year-old operator of the other car were killed. It was only 5:00 p.m.

deprivation: The state of having something taken away.

In an interview after the accident with sleep researcher and authority William C. Dement, M.D., Ph.D., Doucette's father stated that safe driving "was an obsession with Michael." As his father's comment implies, Michael Doucette was a responsible teen who knew much about driver safety. But he overlooked one thing: he hadn't learned about the dangers of sleep **deprivation**. He never considered the possibility of falling asleep at the wheel, and that lack of knowledge killed him.

A good night's sleep is an essential part of good health.

Sleep. It's an important, often ignored, biological need. Oh, we may be quick to take care of other physical needs (we exercise, we eat when we're hungry, we go to the doctor when we're sick), but we often overlook our need for sleep. When we neglect sleep, we end up feeling tired, our minds don't work as well, and sometimes we fall asleep at the wrong times and places. Young Doucette isn't the only one to do so.

According to a recent poll by the National Sleep Foundation, 60 percent of adult drivers in America have driven a vehicle while feeling sleepy. Approximately 37 percent admitted to falling asleep while driving. That means that of almost two hundred million drivers on the road, 117 million of them have driven while sleepy and more than 72 million have actually fallen asleep. Recent studies determined that sleep-related automobile accidents killed more young people than accidents linked to alcohol. Driving sleepy is more dangerous than driving drunk!

But daytime drowsiness isn't only a problem when driving a car. Have you ever fallen asleep in school or on the bus? Have you ever dozed off at work or while trying to read? A recent Gallup survey reports that one out of every two Americans aged eighteen or older complain of chronic daytime drowsiness. Another survey reports that one out of three high school and college students falls asleep in class at least once a week. The National Institutes of Health (NIH) identifies young adults between the ages of twelve and twenty-five as a group at high risk for developing serious sleep problems that can ultimately result in depression, irritability, learning difficulties, weakened memory, and poor school and work performance.

So what's the big deal? you might be tempted wonder. *What difference does it make if I don't get enough sleep? The only person I'm hurting is myself.*

If that's what you think, you couldn't be more wrong.

The results of sleep deprivation don't just affect the person who experiences sleep problems. In Michael Doucette's case, his falling asleep while driving killed another young driver. In some situations, the consequences of insufficient sleep can impact hundreds, even

Our bodies have internal clocks that affect how we perform at various times during a twenty-four hour day. Sleep plays a vital role in keeping our bodies' clocks running smoothly.

Two Essential Features of Sleep

For sleep to be considered sleep (and not unconsciousness, coma, or death) the following two features must be true:

1. Our conscious minds must be essentially unaware of and not perceive the outside world.
2. The condition must be immediately reversible; we must be able to wake up.

thousands, of people. Several major industrial disasters, including the 1979 nuclear meltdown at Pennsylvania's Three Mile Island (the worst nuclear accident in U.S. history) and the massive Alaskan oil spill in 1989, caused by the shipping vessel, Exxon Valdez, are now known to have been partly the result of poor decisions made by experienced workers who had not gotten adequate sleep.

Yes, inadequate sleep is a dangerous thing. One medical professional describes it as "the health crisis" of our day. When we don't get enough sleep, or don't sleep soundly enough, we (and others) suffer the consequences.

What is "enough sleep"? What keeps us from getting enough sleep or the right kind of sleep? Can psychiatric drugs help us sleep better? To answer these questions, we must first understand what sleep is and how it affects us.

What Is Sleep?

We know that sleep is a time of physical rest: Our bodies are generally still; our eyes are usually closed; we're normally lying down and not aware of what's happening around us. Sleep is also a temporary condition; we are able to wake up (unlike if we were in a coma, for example). For sleep to truly be sleep, it must be a reversible state of rest. But what kind of rest does sleep provide?

For centuries, people assumed that sleep happened when all brain activity and consciousness stopped; it was a time when the brain rested. Researchers today know that sleep is something quite different. Thanks to advancements in technology, including the development of the electroencephalograph (EEG) and the polysomnograph, researchers can now measure electrical activity in the brain when a person is asleep.

An EEG is a machine that makes a drawing ("graph") of electrical signals ("electro") generated from the brain ("encephalo"). Electrodes, which are attached by wire to a machine called a galvanometer, are placed on specific points on a person's head where they pick up electrical signals from the person's brain. As the galvanometer reads these signals, ink pens connected to the galvanometer record the signals on graph paper that moves underneath the pens.

A polysomnograph is much like an EEG except that in addition to measuring brain activity, it also measures sleep patterns, waking patterns, and bodily functions like heart rate, muscle activity, and eye movement. Scientists use both machines to study and help people with sleep problems, especially since both procedures help diagnose patients without causing them pain. The electrodes used in both tests may look intimidating, but they only receive electrical signals; they do not send electricity into the person's brain. A patient can sleep comfortably while attached to either machine.

By using EEGs and polysomnographs, researchers have been able to determine that brain activity does not stop during sleep. The brain is actually very active, producing several different types of brain waves. These different brain waves help researchers understand what happens in your brain during different stages of sleep.

Stages of Sleep

When you close your eyes at night and drift off to the Land of Nod, much more is happening in your brain than you realize. The brain is so active during slumber that scientists describe sleep as having an "architecture" all its own. The architecture of sleep consists of two basic types of sleep: a deep, quiet sleep known as non-Rapid Eye Movement (NREM) sleep and a lighter, "dream sleep" called Rapid Eye Movement (REM) sleep, when most dreaming occurs.

NREM sleep has four stages.

Stage One is that drowsy state when you move from being awake to falling asleep. Imagine lying in bed at night: Your eyelids feel heavy; your muscles begin to relax; sounds echo around you, but seem more distant or out of reach; your heart rate and breathing slow down; and though you may be vaguely aware of what's happening around you, you feel yourself drifting away. You've entered Stage One sleep. Stage One sleep normally lasts up to ten minutes (rarely more) and is a state from which you can be easily wakened. If someone were to wake you from Stage One sleep, you might deny that you were sleeping at all.

Stage Two sleep is what many people think of as the first true sleep state, although it is still a very light sleep. Our eyes are closed; our heart and breathing rates slow even more; our muscles become deeply relaxed. We are no longer aware of our surroundings and are truly "asleep." Though this stage lasts only five to twenty minutes, we can still be wakened easily.

Stages Three and Four are the deepest type of sleep and the most difficult from which to wake. On an EEG, these stages show up as the "slow wave sleep" (or delta sleep) characteristic of a deep unconscious state of the mind. This type of sleep deepens as we move from Stage Three to Stage Four, and it provides the kind of rest that best restores our bodies and minds. When we get enough delta sleep we feel refreshed when we wake. We arrive at Stage Three about twenty minutes after lying down and move steadily into the deepest level of sleep, Stage Four, over the next thirty or forty minutes. We reach Stage Four, on average, about an hour after falling into Stage One sleep.

Our sleep architecture does not consist of these four stages alone. They comprise only the quiet phase of our sleep. We also enter the more active REM sleep periodically through the night.

REM Sleep

If you watch someone sleeping, you can tell if they have entered REM sleep by watching their eyes. Beneath the closed eyelids, you can see the circular lump of each eye's raised iris and pupil moving back and forth. The eyes dart from left to right and back again beneath the closed eyelid. This eye shifting occurs only during the part of the sleep cycle called REM sleep.

We enter REM sleep, often called the final stage of sleep, about ninety minutes after we fall asleep. REM sleep begins after we've passed through the deeper sleep stages (Stages Three and Four) and move back into a lighter sleep stage again. Once in a lighter sleep stage, our minds start churning. Scientists believe that REM sleep helps our minds sort through and consolidate our memories and emotions.

REM sleep is the most active sleep phase for our brains, though our bodies remain still. Have you ever awakened during a nightmare but found yourself "frozen" or unable to move? That's because you awoke during REM sleep.

During this part of sleep we dream and interact with our dreams (which is why our eyes dart around), our hearts beat faster and more irregularly, our breathing becomes more rapid, and our blood pressures rise, but we can't move. In her work, *A Woman's Guide to Sleep: Guaranteed Solutions for a Good Night's Rest*, Joyce Walsleben, Ph.D. Director of New York University's School of Medicine's Sleep Disorders Center, notes that our bodies are essentially paralyzed during REM sleep. Only our eyes, hearts, nasal passages, breathing muscles, and erectile tissue can move during this sleep phase. And that's a good thing! Otherwise our bodies would act

During the deepest sleep cycles, our hearts keep beating while much of the rest of our bodies are essentially paralyzed. We need these times of unconsciousness to keep our entire bodies healthy.

out our dreams and not rest! During REM sleep, our brains perform complicated activities while the body stays still.

REM and NREM Sleep: A Complicated Dance

In order to get a good night's sleep and feel rested when we wake, we need to experience all stages of sleep, both REM and NREM. The

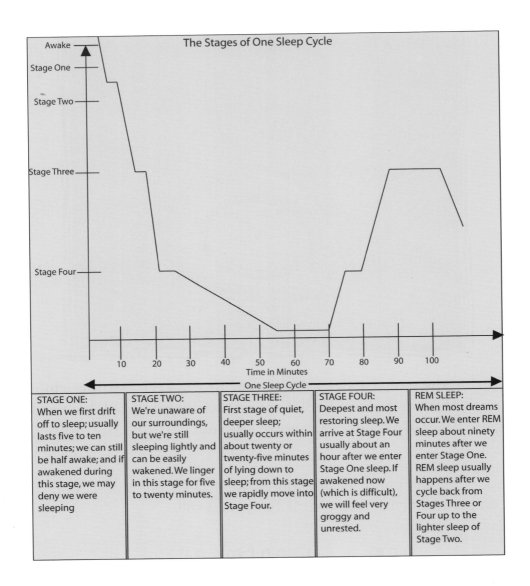

The Stages of One Sleep Cycle

STAGE ONE:
When we first drift off to sleep; usually lasts five to ten minutes; we can still be half awake; and if awakened during this stage, we may deny we were sleeping

STAGE TWO:
We're unaware of our surroundings, but we're still sleeping lightly and can be easily wakened. We linger in this stage for five to twenty minutes.

STAGE THREE:
First stage of quiet, deeper sleep; usually occurs within about twenty or twenty-five minutes of lying down to sleep; from this stage we rapidly move into Stage Four.

STAGE FOUR:
Deepest and most restoring sleep. We arrive at Stage Four usually about an hour after we enter Stage One sleep. If awakened now (which is difficult), we will feel very groggy and unrested.

REM SLEEP:
When most dreams occur. We enter REM sleep about ninety minutes after we enter Stage One. REM sleep usually happens after we cycle back from Stages Three or Four up to the lighter sleep of Stage Two.

four NREM stages described above plus REM sleep combine to make up what scientists call "sleep cycles." We complete the first sleep cycle when we pass from Stage One through Stages Two, Three, and Four, then back to a lighter stage where REM sleep occurs. The sleep we experience from the time we slip into Stage One to when we complete our first REM sleep is considered our first sleep cycle. The time from the end of our first REM sleep to the end of our second REM sleep (including all the stages in between) is the second cycle. From the end of that REM sleep to the end of the next is the third, and so on.

Most people go through four or five sleep cycles during a normal night's sleep, each cycle lasting, on average, about ninety to one hundred minutes. These cycles, however, vary. Though each cycle contains all stages of sleep, cycles during the earlier part of our night contain more deep sleep, while cycles toward the end of our night's rest contain more REM sleep (and more dreams). That's why we often recall dreams when we wake in the morning.

This complicated interplay between REM sleep, NREM sleep, and sleep cycles seems like it happens effortlessly. It's as though our bodies know the steps to a complicated dance and follow the rhythm where it leads, without having to think about it. What enables our bodies to follow the dance is an internal twenty-four-hour clock that tells us when to sleep and when to wake. This internal clock is called our circadian rhythm ("circa" means "about," "dian" means "day"). When our internal clock says it's time to sleep, our body processes slow down and we feel sleepy. When our internal clock says its time to be active, we wake up and our body processes kick back into gear.

Because sleep is such a complicated process, many things can go wrong:

We can have difficulty falling asleep.
We can have difficulty staying asleep.
We can have difficulty making it through all the sleep stages.
We can get too much REM sleep and not enough NREM sleep.
We can have difficulty waking up.
We can fall asleep at the wrong times or in the wrong places.

Consequences of Poor Sleep

According to the National Sleep Foundation, adolescents who don't get enough sleep or don't experience regular restful sleep are more prone to:

Unintentional injuries and death (from accidents).
Low grades and poor school performance.
Negative moods (anger, sadness, depression, fear, etc.).
Substance abuse (caffeine, nicotine, prescription drugs, illegal drugs, and alcohol).

We can wake up too soon.
We can sleep too long.
We can sleep restlessly or poorly.
Our body clocks can be wrong.

Both quantity (how much we sleep) and quality (what stages of sleep we reach and how long we spend there) are important when it comes to getting the sleep we need. Only when we enter all sleep cycles at appropriate times, and stay long enough in Stages Three and Four, will we feel refreshed.

No one can say if it was the quantity of his sleep or the quality that made him so tired, but in either case, Michael Doucette didn't get the kind of sleep he needed, and it cost him his life. Even though he probably only entered Stage One sleep when he dozed while driving that February afternoon, it was enough to cause him to lose control of his car and collide with another. If only Michael had been as obsessive about getting the right kind of sleep as he was about being safe in his driving, it might have saved two lives.

How about you? Think about your own sleep habits. Are you making sure you're getting enough sleep? Do you know how much sleep you need? What kind of sleep are you getting? Are you entering all stages of sleep? Do you enjoy several full cycles of sleep each night? Bear in mind as you weigh these questions that each of us is different. What is a "normal" night's sleep for you may be completely different from a normal night's sleep for someone else.

What Is Normal for You?

We've all heard that eight hours is the recommended amount of sleep for health and well-being. We've also heard that our eight hours should occur between 10:00 p.m. and 6:00 a.m. Today's sleep researchers know that while eight hours might be sufficient for some, it is hardly best for all people. In fact, researchers have learned that there are different types of sleep personalities. Harvard Medical School professor, Dr. Martin Moore-Ede, a world-renowned expert on sleep, fatigue, and human alertness, has identified three primary sleep personalities (using bird species for his labels):

- The Lark: an early riser and early to bed-er; morning is her best time of day.
- The Owl: a night person; the later, the better, but mornings are impossible.
- The Regular Robin: doesn't wake too early or stay up too late; thinks Owls and Larks are strange.

If you're an Owl, you probably won't be able to fall asleep at 10:00 p.m., no matter how hard you try. If you're a Lark, sleeping until 7:00 a.m. will be too late for you. The standard recommended bed times

Sleeping Away Our Lives?

Assuming an average of eight hours of sleep per day, most people spend a third of their lives in slumber land! That means that by the time you reach fifteen years of age, five of your years will have been spent catching some zzzzz's. By the time you reach seventy-five years of age, you will have slept twenty-five years (9,125 days or 219,000 hours). But that's not so bad. Some armadillos, opossums, and sloths spend as much as 80 percent of their lives sleeping!

may not fit your body's natural sleep rhythms, so it's important to understand your sleep personality. Which personality are you?

People's sleep needs, however, don't just vary by sleep personality. They also vary by quantity: how much sleep is needed. Some people are short sleepers who can get by on five hours of sleep every night and not feel sleep deprived. Others need nine hours of sleep per night to function well.

How much sleep do you need? One way to tell is by how you feel when you wake. If you get up on your own (no alarm clock) feeling refreshed (not tired or groggy), and you get through your day without feeling chronically sleepy, you've probably gotten the right amount of sleep.

Other factors can influence how much sleep we need: the environment where we sleep (room lighting, noise, etc.); our exercise or fitness levels; eating and drinking habits; illness or other medical problems; psychological problems; pressure, worries, or fears. But even when we have all these factors in place—even when we know

We all need our nightly dreams in order to renew ourselves physically, mentally, and emotionally.

Not enough sleep can leave us feeling groggy and headachy the next day.

Don't Try This at Home!

In January 1965, San Diego high school student Randy Gardner set a new world record for the longest continuous time without sleep: 264 hours. The eighteen-year-old student stayed awake (with much help from family, friends, and sleep researchers Dr. William C. Dement and Dr. George Gulevich) for *eleven days straight* as part of a study on sleep deprivation.

our sleep personality and how much sleep we need—we can still experience sleep troubles. The root of our sleeplessness may not be any of those things but may be something else entirely. We may have a sleep disorder.

Just as the earth experiences a daily cycle of light and dark, our bodies require cycles of both wakefulness and sleep.

Chapter Two

A Brief Overview of Sleep Disorders

Sixteen-year-old Susan heard the high-pitched, piercing scream and at first did nothing. Resting her forehead on her hand, she shook her head, and closed her eyes.

I'm never going to get this lab report done. Not tonight, anyway. She sighed, closed her notebook, got up, and sauntered to her younger brother's room, from where she'd heard the scream. Susan's parents had gone out for the evening, and the high school junior was babysitting her young sibling. She knew what she'd find when she opened his door.

Just as Susan expected, seven-year-old Willie was sitting straight up in his bed, eyes wide with terror. His breathing and sweating made him look like he'd just run a hundred-yard dash, but his dazed expression told his sister that he was still asleep. Susan recognized that Willie was genuinely terrified, but there was little she could do. From experience, the responsible teenager knew not to wake him; he'd only be confused and wouldn't recall what troubled his sleep. Willie's fear had to run its course. Then he'd settle down and sleep peacefully for the rest of the night. For his safety, Susan had to sit with him until then. Sometimes, if frightened enough, Willie would bolt out of bed and run out of the house. Sometimes, he hurt himself as he fled.

Susan's chemistry report would have to wait. She needed to stay with Willie.

Night terrors can disrupt an entire family's sleep.

A poor night's sleep can interfere with work performance the next day.

If you heard a bloodcurdling scream early in the night, would you react as calmly as Susan did? You might if you had a younger sibling who regularly experienced night terrors. Certainly, Susan wasn't always so calm. When Willie first started his screaming episodes, the entire family responded with fear and worry that bordered on panic. What disturbed them most was that they couldn't wake him from his awful nightmares. Willie, they soon learned however, wasn't experiencing nightmares. He had a sleep disorder.

night terrors: A condition in which a person, while in deep, non-dreaming sleep, screams and displays other terrified actions.

Primary Sleep Disorders

The Diagnostic and Statistical Manual of Mental Disorders, fourth edition, text revision (DSM-IV-TR) divides primary sleep disorders into two groups:

1. dyssomnias (problems with quantity, quality, or time of sleep), which include:

   primary insomnia
   primary hypersomnia
   narcolepsy
   breathing-related sleep disorder
   circadian rhythm sleep disorder
   dyssomnias not otherwise specified

2. parasomnias (problems with behavior during sleep), which include:

   nightmare disorder
   sleep terror disorder
   sleepwalking disorder
   parasomnias not otherwise specified

Sleep Disorders

Everyone occasionally has difficulty falling asleep, especially when stressed. Have you ever worried about a major project or upcoming exam? Chances are you didn't sleep well the night before it was due. Have you ever eaten out late and enjoyed a café latte with dessert?

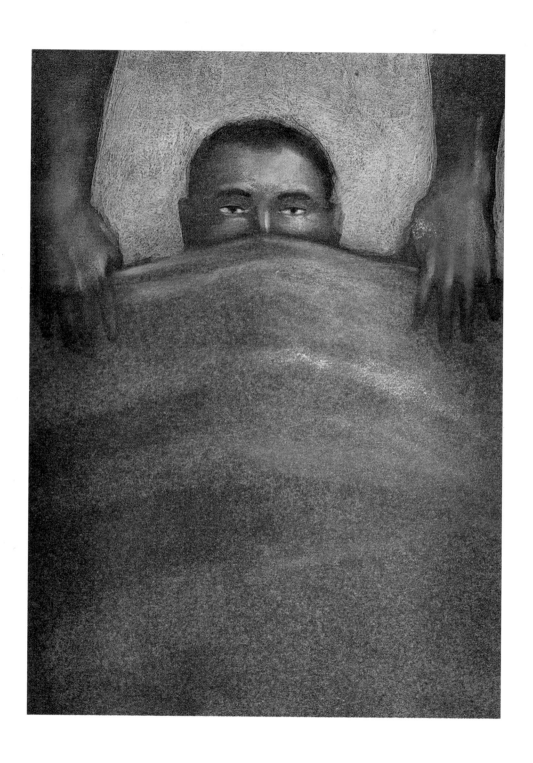

The caffeine and sugar probably made it difficult to fall asleep when you got home. Have you ever had a bad cold? Coughing or congestion may have wakened you during the night. We all face these sleep difficulties sometime in our lives; they are no cause for alarm. But when problems with sleep become chronic, disrupt our normal routine, or interfere with our ability to work, go to school, or act appropriately, we may have a sleep disorder.

The International Classification of Sleep Disorders, Diagnostic and Coding Manual, published by the American Sleep Disorders Association, lists more than eighty different sleep disorders! How can a doctor know which disorder you have, especially when so many of the disorders listed closely resemble other disorders?

Medical professionals use a reference book called the *Diagnostic and Statistical Manual of Mental Disorders*, currently the fourth edition, text revision (DSM-IV-TR), to diagnose sleep disorders. Although there are too many sleep disorders for us to discuss in detail here, the DSM-IV-TR lists primary sleep disorders as sleep disruptions that are not caused by illness, injuries, mental disorders, or other medical conditions. Medications, abusing drugs, or drinking

Bedtime routines can help us settle down at night—but sleep disorders can interfere with a good night's sleep.

Do You Have a Sleep Disorder?

You might have insomnia if you . . .
- have difficulty falling asleep.
- can't stay asleep.
- wake up too early.
- feel tired all day.

You might have obstructive sleep apnea if you . . .
- are overweight.
- snore loudly, snort, or gasp in your sleep.
- wake up feeling tired and feel sleepy all day.

You might have restless leg syndrome if you . . .
- experience uncomfortable "creepy-crawly" sensations in your legs.
- need to kick, shake, or stretch your legs to get rid of the sensation.
- notice that your discomfort increases when you rest or lie still.

You might have delayed sleep phase syndrome if you . . .
- regularly can't fall asleep until 3:00 a.m. or 4:00 a.m.
- find it almost impossible to get up in the morning.
- sleep in very late on days you don't have to get up.

alcohol, though they can disrupt sleep, cannot be the source of a sleep difficulty for it to be labeled a primary sleep disorder. For a sleep disturbance to be called a primary sleep disorder it must be caused by abnormalities in a person's sleep/wake patterns or timing.

The DSM-IV-TR divides primary sleep disorders into two subgroups: dyssomnias, which include disorders stemming from the amount, quality, or timing of sleep, and parasomnias, which are characterized by abnormal behaviors while a person is sleeping.

Dyssomnias

If you have trouble falling asleep, or with how much (or how little) you sleep, how deeply you sleep, or when you sleep, you may be struggling with a dyssomnia.

When You're Not Able to Sleep

Imagine lying on your back in bed staring at the ceiling. The red glow of your digital clock tells you it's 2:00 a.m. The house is still. The road outside is void of traffic. The only sound you hear is the quiet ticking of the grandfather clock in the hall. You sigh, glance at your bedside clock again, and then roll onto your side in an attempt to get comfortable enough to fall asleep. Nope. No good. You turn over once more, rustling the covers with you as you move. It's no use. Tomorrow will be another exhausted day, just like most other days of the last six weeks. Why can't you fall asleep?

Insomnia, which is chronic difficulty falling asleep or staying asleep, is one of the most well-known dyssomnias listed in the DSM-IV-TR. Since a person with insomnia doesn't get sufficient rest at night, he is often sleepy during the day. Excessive daytime sleepiness is a primary symptom of insomnia.

When worried or excited, many people experience difficulty getting to sleep for a night or two, even for a week or more. Many children, even adolescents, sometimes find it difficult to go to sleep Christmas Eve because they're excited about what awaits them the

The presents waiting under the tree may keep children awake on Christmas Eve!

People with sleep disorders may lose their tempers easily.

next morning. Teens often find it nearly impossible to sleep the night before they take their driver's test. In these cases, although those involved have difficulty going to sleep because circumstances create stress, these sleep troubles aren't a true sleep disorder. For a sleep disturbance to be considered primary insomnia, as it's listed in the DSM-IV-TR, it must last longer than a few weeks and must cause poor sleep almost every night for at least a month.

When You Sleep Too Much

The inability to fall asleep or stay asleep isn't the only trouble a person can have with sleep. Sometimes people can sleep too much. In the DSM-IV-TR, this need to sleep too much is called primary hypersomnia ("hyper" means "excessive," "somnia" or "somnus" means "sleep"). People with primary hypersomnia tend to fall asleep quickly and stay asleep for a long time. They can be very difficult to wake. They can also be grumpy or groggy for a long time after waking. No matter how much sleep these people get, they continue to feel drowsy and lethargic. No amount of sleep will help them feel energetic or refreshed.

People with primary hypersomnia often take naps during the day. Sometimes they plan to nap; other times they fall asleep when they don't mean to. Unintentionally falling asleep during the day can lead to problems in school (the person might be viewed as lazy) or at work (she might be considered irresponsible).

Primary hypersomnia usually first appears between the ages of fifteen and thirty, and comes on gradually. Without treatment it can become an ongoing condition.

When You Experience "Sleep Attacks"

Even more dangerous than not being able to fall asleep or sleeping too much is a condition called narcolepsy. This dyssomnia is a sleep disorder that involves a sudden, irresistible attack of REM sleep (the dreaming stage of sleep) during normal waking hours. As we discussed in chapter 1, normal REM sleep follows the first four stages of NREM sleep; it is during the sleep phase that the mind is active but the body is still; we are essentially paralyzed during REM sleep. A person with narcolepsy skips the first four stages of sleep and jumps immediately into REM sleep, often with no warning. Because he enters a REM state so quickly (skipping the other stages), a person with narcolepsy may enter REM sleep before his brain is fully asleep: He can actually be dreaming while he is awake. These "awake dreams" seem real and usually occur just before falling asleep or immediately on waking, but they are only hallucinations. What seems real is not. It's only a dream. On waking, he may also struggle with sleep paralysis, a period of seconds or minutes when he can't move or speak.

hallucinations: Imagined sensations that are heard, seen, or smelled, with no basis in reality.

The person with narcolepsy doesn't only hallucinate and experience momentary paralysis, he can also experience a condition called cataplexy, when, though fully conscious, he suddenly

Not Every Sleep Trouble Is a Sleep Disorder

All the following can disrupt your sleep, but they do not cause, nor are they considered, sleep disorders:

- Worry: when your anxiety, fear, or nervousness keeps you awake.
- Poor sleep habits: when you regularly stay up late or go to sleep at irregular times.
- Poor lifestyle habits: exercising right before bed or abusing drugs, cigarettes, or alcohol.
- Daytime napping: when you sleep too much during the day to be able to sleep at night.
- Poor sleep environment: when your bed is uncomfortable or your bedroom is too hot, too cold, too noisy, or has too much light.
- Eating habits: when stimulants like caffeine and sugar keep you awake.
- Colds and allergies: when a stuffy nose or cough disturbs your sleep.
- Psychiatric challenges: when something like depression keeps you awake.

loses muscle strength and control (ranging in severity from slight weakness to complete collapse). Cataplexy can happen anywhere at any time, making this condition extremely dangerous. Think of how disastrous it could be to lose control of your body while swimming or driving a car! Although cataplexy can happen spontaneously, it usually happens in response to strong emotions including anger, surprise, laughter, and extreme excitement.

A person with narcolepsy can experience "sleep attacks" any-where—while shopping, playing soccer, having a conversation, or taking notes in class. An attack may come while walking across the street, riding a bike, or mowing the lawn. This makes the condition not only dangerous but also embarrassing and terrifying to live with.

When You Can't Breathe Well While You Sleep

As dangerous as narcolepsy is, another dyssomnia, which, if serious and left untreated, can be fatal: breathing-related sleep disorder. In his classic reference, *The Promise of Sleep*, world-renowned sleep authority William C. Dement, M.D., defines sleep apnea (a breath-ing-related sleep disorder) as an "unrecognized killer." If you suffer from this disorder you actually stop breathing while you sleep—sometimes for a few seconds, sometimes for a minute or more.

Dr. Dement likens the breathing stoppage process to a straw. Imagine putting your finger over one end of a straw, then sucking on the other end. What happens? The straw collapses; it flattens out. In people with apnea, a similar process happens in their throats. As they suck air in, the walls of the throat start to collapse, shutting off the airway. They can't breathe. This breathing stoppage can happen as many as dozens of times per hour or hundreds of times per night.

According to the National Sleep Association, 12 million Ameri-cans stop breathing this way every night! Some die. Most wake mo-mentarily when they choke or snore to begin breathing again on their own, but then fall immediately back to sleep. Nearly all awaken the next morning exhausted, with no recollection of the breathing difficulty.

When Your Sleep Clock Is Off or You Can't Stay Still

Sometimes our problems with sleep have nothing to do with breath-ing difficulties or getting too much (or too little) sleep. When this is the case, our sleep difficulty may have more to do with our internal clock.

As we discussed in chapter 1, we all have a clock inside us that provides a healthy pattern of sleeping and waking for our bodies. We have a natural timer, called our circadian rhythm, which directs when we sleep and wake. For most of us, our body clock tells us to sleep at night and to be active during the day. Circadian rhythm disorder (once called sleep–wake schedule disorder) involves a disruption to that clock: either the clock is delayed, and the person can't sleep until later at night and can't get up until later in the morning; or it is moved up, and the person needs to go to sleep and wake up much earlier than normal.

The DSM-IV-TR suggests that as many as seven percent of adolescents have the delayed circadian rhythm disorder called delayed sleep phase syndrome (DSPS). This explains why so many young people find it nearly impossible to fall asleep until two or three o'clock in the morning and are unable to wake before early afternoon.

When Your Legs Can't Stay Still

One last group of dyssomnias include sleep disruptions that occur when our bodies just can't stay still. Have you ever been drifting off to sleep when your legs suddenly jerk as if you tripped over something? Or have your feet or arms ever felt so tingly or itchy that you need to move them to relieve the uncomfortable sensations? Periodic limb movements and restless legs syndrome (RLS) can prevent an individual from falling asleep or sleeping peacefully and can result in excessive daytime fatigue.

Parasomnias

So far we've looked at problems that occur in the mechanics of sleep: things that affect the ability to fall asleep, stay asleep, or sleep at the right times. Another set of sleep disturbances can rob us of sleep as well. Instead of impacting how we sleep, these disturbances, called parasomnias, affect what we do while we sleep.

When Dreams Frighten

Thirteen-year-old Mary didn't move. She watched silently as the darkly dressed man climbed through her open bedroom window. Her curtains' sheer panels billowed softly in the breeze as the threatening figure drew nearer to her four-poster bed. With heart pounding, she gripped her comforter tightly to her chest and tried to scream. But no sound came. Her throat tightened and her eyes widened with helpless fear as she watched the stranger reach his gloved hand toward her face. *Nooooooooo!* Her silent call echoed in her brain as she felt the pressure of his smothering grip. *I don't want to die!*

Then she awoke.

Though this episode seemed real, Mary was never in any real danger. She was having a nightmare. She could recall every detail of her terrifying ordeal when she woke up, but though she was alert and aware of her surroundings, her fear lingered. It was difficult for her to go back to sleep.

According to the DSM-IV-TR, nightmares are very common. As many as one out of two adults report having an occasional nightmare that disrupts their sleep. Young adults can have nightmares more frequently. When a person has nightmares that repeat themselves or happen often enough to cause significant distress or disruption of ordinary life, that person is said to have a nightmare disorder.

Terror Without Dreams

Sleep terror disorder is different than nightmare disorder, though the two are often confused. What's the difference? Nightmares happen during that dreaming stage called REM sleep. The person's waking fear and anxiety is related to dreams they remember and can describe. Sleep terrors happen during non-REM sleep. The person cannot recall any dreams to explain his fear.

Sleep terrors often begin with a scream or panicked cry that occurs shortly after falling asleep. The person usually does not awaken (and will be difficult to wake if you try) and has no recall of the event when she gets up in the morning. During a typical sleep terror, a person will abruptly sit up, scream or cry, breath rapidly, sweat profusely, and will be unresponsive to those around her. She often cannot be comforted.

If you waken someone during a sleep terror, he will be confused and disoriented, not alert. Most of the time, he won't wake fully but will return to sleep. Whether you waken someone with sleep terrors or not, he may attempt to "escape" from whatever terrifies him. This escape can often take the form of sleepwalking.

When We Walk, Talk, and Eat in Our Sleep

While sleepwalking, a person who is still asleep can rise from her bed and walk about the room, down the stairs, or even leave the home. She can do simple things like eat, talk, go to the bathroom, and open or close doors. She will generally have a blank look on her face and be unresponsive to other people if they attempt to communicate with her. It is very difficult to wake someone who is sleepwalking, and if you do, she will not recall getting up or moving around.

According to the DSM-IV-TR, sleepwalking (also called somnambulism) usually begins between the ages of four and eight but peaks when a person reaches her preteen years, usually by age twelve. These episodes generally disappear by the time the sleepwalker reaches fifteen years of age, but in some cases, they continue into adulthood.

When We Can't Move

One last parasomnia can be even more terrifying than the rest: sleep paralysis. We discussed sleep paralysis as part of narcolepsy earlier in this chapter, because it often occurs with that sleep disorder, but sleep paralysis is a parasomnia that can occur on its own.

While sleeping or when you just wake up, have you ever felt you were suffocating or as though someone were standing over you, but you couldn't move? You felt completely awake, but you couldn't speak or do anything. This inability to move is called sleep paralysis. If you've ever experienced this, you know how frightening it can be.

Thankfully, for most people, sleep paralysis is a normal, passing occurrence that will diminish on its own without medical intervention. But like each of the sleep problems listed here, it can become severe enough to cause emotional distress. Or it can manifest itself as part of another problem. When it does, sleep paralysis is treated as a sleep disorder.

The Good News: Sleep Disorders Can Be Helped

In our discussion of sleep difficulties so far, we've barely scratched the surface of the number and combination of possible sleep disruptions. Instead, we've focused on those problems with sleep that the DSM-IV-TR classifies as primary sleep disorders (there are others). These disorders are medical conditions that should not be taken lightly. Whether your sleep disorder is a dyssomnia that impacts the quantity, quality, or timing of your sleep, or a parasomnia that affects your behavior while sleeping, it is a condition that can seriously disrupt your life, health, and emotional well-being. You need to seek help.

The good news is that doctors can successfully treat most primary sleep disorders. While drug treatment plays only a limited role in treating most of these disorders, prescription drugs can play an important role in overcoming problems with sleep.

The evil stepmother's poison apple was the cause of Snow White's slumber.

Chapter Three

Sleep Drugs Past and Present

Sometimes they just fell asleep.

Sometimes a god was called on to induce their slumber.

Sometimes a poisoned apple or sewing spindle did the trick.

Sometimes a magic brew was used to cause sleep.

And sometimes it was a field of brilliant red flowers.

Whatever the method, characters from literature past and present experienced many sleeps:

Poor "Joe, the fat boy," from nineteenth-century English novelist Charles Dickens' *Pickwick Papers*, was so drowsy he often dozed off while standing.

In Greek mythology, Hera, the great god Zeus' wife, enlisted the aid of Hypnos, the god of sleep, to put her mighty husband to sleep.

In the early 1800s, the Brothers Grimm fairy-tale heroines Snow White and Sleeping Beauty fell prey to poisoned apples and sleep-inducing sewing spindle spells.

Washington Irving's delightfully lazy, henpecked character Rip Van Winkle sipped frothy mugs of unknown brew, then slumbered in the Catskill Mountains for twenty years.

Decades later, in 1900, the Wicked Witch of the West, in L. Frank Baum's *The Wizard of Oz*, used a bewitched poppy field to put Dorothy, Toto, and their friends to sleep on their way to the Land of Oz.

Our literature reflects our curiosity about sleep. Sleep theories have fascinated us for centuries. What causes sleep? What is sleep? What can be done for people who can't sleep? The answers to these questions have been the subject of much speculation. Advances in medicine and technology over the last century have begun to provide a scientific understanding of sleep that is unlike any in the past.

Just as sleep theories have abounded, so have sleep treatments. The Greek god of sleep, Hypnos, was usually depicted as a young man with wings on his shoulders or protruding from his temples holding opium in one hand and a poppy plant in the other. Opium, which comes from the poppy, was one of the earliest sleep treatment drugs.

Early Drug Treatments

Opium is a narcotic drug prepared from the poppy plant. Its "magical" ability to cause sleep and to make a person feel "high" or "joyful" made it a valuable trade item for ancient civilizations. As early as 3400 BCE, opium was grown and harvested in Mesopotamia. The Sumerians, Assyrians, Egyptians, Phoenicians, Minoans, Romans, and

A nineteenth-century drawing portrays the "monsters" that arise in our sleeping minds.

other ancient peoples used opium for its medicinal effects. It was often used as a sleep aid for those who were unable to sleep because of sicknesses or injury.

In 460 BCE, Hippocrates, the "father of medicine," affirmed that opium was not a magic potion but a medicinal plant that could be used to treat illness, injury, and disease. It could help patients rest who otherwise could not do so.

It wasn't until 1753 CE that the opium poppy was officially classified. Swedish plant expert Carl Linnaeus, the father of modern botany, named the plant "Papaver somniferum," which means "sleep-inducing."

Though opium induced sleep and caused feelings of euphoria, it was also highly addictive. Opium addiction became a huge problem

DR. R.C. FLOWER'S
Nerve Pills
THE
GREAT BRAIN & NERVE FOOD, WILL QUICKLY OVERCOME
Sleeplessness, Restlessness, Hysteria, &c.

GEO. N. ALLING,
GRAND AVE. cor. STATE ST., NEW HAVEN, CONN.

Dr. Flower's nerve pills were advertised as a cure for sleeplessness and restlessness.

A Partial Time Line of Sleep Aids

3400 BCE: Opium. Ancient civilizations thought this plant had magical properties.

460 BCE: Opium. Hippocrates, the father of modern medicine, rejects the "magic" idea but affirms opium's medicinal properties.

5 BCE–5 CE: Greek mythology taught that sleep came from Hypnos, the god of sleep.

1700–1800s: Opium use leads to widespread addiction in Europe.

1827: Morphine is manufactured to combat opium addiction and sleep problems.

1861: Morphine is used in the U.S. Civil War as an anesthetic for battlefield surgery.

1903: Barbiturates are first introduced in the United States. They become the drug of choice for treating insomnia for the first half of the twentieth century.

1931: Stimulants are first used to treat narcolepsy.

1950s and 1960s: Barbiturates develop their deadly reputation because of the number of Hollywood celebrities who used them in suicide attempts.

1970s: Doctors begin prescribing a safer class of sleep aid: the benzodiazepines. These are used to treat insomnia, sleep terrors, and sleepwalking disorders.

1992: The imidazopyridine Ambien, a safe, nonaddictive sleep aid with minimal side effects, is approved by the U.S. FDA for use in the United States. It becomes the new drug of choice for treating insomnia.

1998: The FDA approves a new drug, modafinil, to treat narcolepsy. It's the first drug developed in more than forty years specifically to treat daytime sleepiness.

in late eighteenth-century and early nineteenth-century Europe. To ease the problem of opium addiction, another poppy-related drug was developed—morphine. In 1827, German pharmaceutical company E. Merck & Company began the commercial manufacture of morphine not only to treat opium addiction but for use as a painkiller and sleep aid. By the start of the U.S. Civil War in 1861, morphine was a commonly used anesthetic; it put people to sleep so doctors could perform painless surgery on the battlefield.

Unfortunately, morphine also was addictive. One historian notes that by the end of the nineteenth century, more than 400,000 people had the "army disease"—morphine addiction.

Drug Regulations and Newer Sleep Aids

By the early 1900s, the U.S. government stepped in. In 1905, the U.S. government banned opium sales. In 1906, the U.S. Congress passed the Pure Food and Drug Act, requiring all medicines to be accurately labeled. The new labeling law required any addictive substances, including the presence of opiates (opium and morphine), found in medicines to be listed on the medicine's package and label. When people discovered that their medicines contained addictive substances (something they didn't know before the labeling laws), many stopped buying these drugs.

In 1914, another law, the Harrison Narcotics Act, made it illegal to possess narcotics or other addictive drugs (including morphine, opium, heroin, and cocaine) unless a physician prescribed them. Because of this and other new laws, opium-based drugs became harder to obtain. By 1915, opiates were no longer legal, and sleep-deprived people turned to a different class of drugs, called **hypnotics**, to aid their sleep.

hypnotics: A class of drugs that cause a person to sleep or to enter a hypnosis-like state.

Researchers are continuing to explore new substances that can affect the brain's sleep mechanisms.

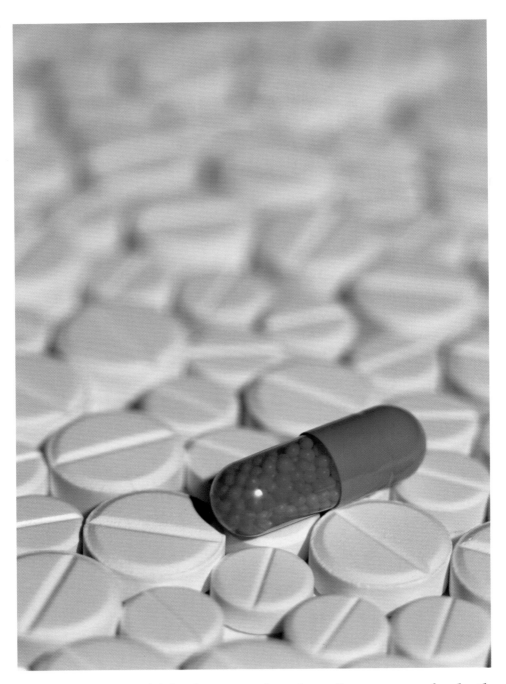

The modern world looks to medications for answers for both physical and mental disorders.

The Hypnotics

Hypnotics were drugs that seemed to hypnotize people; they put people to sleep. A drug named barbital (named so because it was made from barbituric acid) was first introduced in the United States in 1903 and became one of the most widely used hypnotics of the early twentieth century. Doctors initially used the drug as a tranquilizer to calm anxious patients, but its ability to induce sleep soon became widely known. By the early 1920s, barbital (also known as Veronal) and a related drug, phenobarbital (also called Luminal) were the drugs of choice to combat sleep problems. But they, too, had the potential to cause harm.

barbiturates: A highly addictive class of sleeping pills first developed in the early 1900s.

Just as opium and morphine caused addictions, barbital, phenobarbital, and other **barbiturates** created dependency in those who took them. Once again people became addicted to their sleeping pills. Even worse than addiction, barbiturates posed an additional danger: they resulted in death if you took too many or mixed them with alcohol. In the early 1940s, a magazine published by the American Medical Association ran an article warning readers about the addictive nature and possible abuse of barbiturates and recommended that people use these drugs only under a doctor's care.

Until the mid-twentieth century, those who needed drug treatment for sleep disturbances could find help only in dangerous, highly addictive chemicals. Would this always be the case? Thankfully, no.

Modern Drug Treatment: The Benzodiazepines

By the 1970s, a new class of sleeping pill was developed: the benzodiazepines. This class of drugs was used (and still is used) to treat

Common Prescription Drugs Used for Sleeping Disorders

Drug Class	Chemical Name	Trade Name	Usual Adult Daily Dosage
Benzodiaz-epines	alprazolam	Xanax	0.25–1.0 mg., 3x/day
	chlordiaz-epoxide	Librium	5–25 mg., 3-4x/day
	diazepam	diazepam	2–10 mg., 2–4x/day
	flurazepam	Dalmane	15–30 mg
	estazolam	ProSom	1–2 mg.
	lorazepam	Ativan	2–4 mg.
	temazepam	Restoril	15–30 mg.
	triazolam	Halcion	0.125–0.25 mg.
Imidazopyri-dines:	zolpidem tar-trate	Ambien	10 mg.
Pyrazolopy-rimidines:	zaleplon	Sonata	5–10 mg.
Antidepres-sants:	amitriptyline	Elavil	25–50 mg.
	trazodone	Desyrel	50–100 mg.
Antihista-mines:	hydroxyzine	Atarax	50 mg.
	hydroxyzine	Vistaril	50 mg.

anxiety and panic disorders, but it is also an effective sleep aid. Benzodiazepines help a person fall asleep faster and sleep longer.

Because benzodiazepines' action on the brain prevents a person from reaching Stage Four sleep, doctors today use this class of drugs to treat night terrors and sleepwalking, which occur only during the deepest sleep stage. If you can prevent a person from entering a certain sleep stage, and certain disorders only happen during that stage, then, the thinking goes, eliminating the sleep stage should eliminate the disorder. This drug treatment usually works.

Most benzodiazepines are known better by their trade names (the names the manufacturers sell them under): Dalmane, Librium, Restoril, Halcion, and ProSom. The best-known benzodiazepine is probably diazepam, otherwise known as Valium; other benzodiazepines that are often used to treat anxiety are Klonopin, Ativan, and Xanax. Though these medications are primarily used to treat anxiety, doctors sometimes use them for insomnia as well. Many benzodiazepines are still in use today.

All sedatives, however, including benzodiazepines, can cause psychological and physiological dependence. Addiction is only a danger, though, when these drugs are abused or when they are not taken as directed by the prescribing practitioner. Benzodiazepines are typically used on a short-term basis only, while waiting for a slower acting medication to take effect.

The New Hypnotics

These new drugs often replaced barbiturates, since most barbiturates were addictive, dangerous drugs that could be deadly when you took too much. They were often the drug of choice for attempted (and successful) suicide. Because of their propensity to kill and their highly addictive nature, barbiturates aren't used much today. But benzodiazepines didn't replace the other hypnotics. In fact, a new, safer class of hypnotics has been developed in recent years, called imidazopyridines.

Drug Approval

Before a drug can be marketed in the United States, it must be officially approved by the Food and Drug Administration (FDA). Today's FDA is the primary consumer protection agency in the United States. Operating under the authority given it by the government, and guided by laws established throughout the twentieth century, the FDA has established a rigorous drug approval process that verifies the safety, effectiveness, and accuracy of labeling for any drug marketed in the United States.

While the United States has the FDA for the approval and regulation of drugs and medical devices, Canada has a similar organization called the Therapeutic Product Directorate (TPD). The TPD is a division of Health Canada, the Canadian government department of health. The TPD regulates drugs, medical devices, disinfectants, and sanitizers with disinfectant claims. Some of the things that the TPD monitors are quality, effectiveness, and safety. Just as the FDA must approve new drugs in the United States, the TPD must approve new drugs in Canada before those drugs can enter the market.

The most popular drug in this new hypnotic class is zolpidem tartrate, or Ambien. Marketed in Europe since 1987, Ambien was approved by the FDA for use in the United States in 1992 and has become the most-used drug to treat insomnia.

Ambien: A Study in How a Sleep Drug Works

Eighteen-year-old Kelly enjoyed her three-week exchange trip to China. As a college freshman, she went to Beijing to study the Chi-

Brand Names vs. Generic Names

Talking about psychiatric drugs can be confusing, because every drug has at least two names: its "generic name" and the "brand name" that the pharmaceutical company uses to market the drug. Generic names come from the drugs' chemical structures, while brand names are used by drug companies in order to inspire public recognition and loyalty for their products.

Here are the brand names and generic names for some common drugs used for treating sleep disorders:

Ambien®	zolpidem
Atarax®	hydroxyzine
Ativan®	lorazepam
Benadryl®	diphenhydramine
Dalmane®	flurazepam
Desyrel®	trazodone
Elavil®	amitriptyline
Halcion®	triazolam
Klonopin®	clonazepam
Librium®	chlordiazepoxide
ProSom®	estazolam
Restoril®	temazepam
Sonata®	zaleplon
Vistaril®	hydroxyzine
Valium®	diazepam
Xanax®	alprazolam

If Your Doctor Prescribes a "Sleeping Pill"

Doctors and other sleep medicine experts recommend that you follow these guidelines if you take medication to help you sleep:

- Make sure your doctor knows what other drugs, herbs, or vitamins you are taking.
- When you take a prescribed sleeping pill, use the lowest dosage possible.
- Never take more than your doctor prescribes.
- Take the pill according to your doctor's recommended timing.
- Do not take sleeping pills after midnight.
- After taking a sleep medication, do not drive or operate machinery.
- If you take a sleep aid, do not drink alcohol or abuse drugs.
- Never give your sleeping pills to someone else.
- Use sleeping pills only for a short time (a maximum of ten days).
- If you experience unexpected side effects, call your doctor immediately.

nese language and culture, but she most enjoyed her part-time responsibility teaching Chinese nationals the English language.

"They're an incredibly gentle, gracious people," Kelly enthused when she returned. "They gave me far more than I ever could have given them. The whole trip was a life-changing experience." But no one prepared Kelly for how difficult her return to America would be.

When Kelly returned, her body clock (that internal rhythm of waking and sleeping) was still tuned to Beijing time. But Beijing's time zone is thirteen hours ahead of Kelly's hometown outside of New York City. When it was 9:00 a.m. in New York (the start of a normal workday), it was 10:00 p.m. in China (time for bed). When it was bedtime in New York, the day was just beginning in Beijing. After returning to the United States, Kelly couldn't fall asleep at night because her body clock told her it wasn't really night time; it was morning (in Beijing). Several weeks after return-

ing home, Kelly still couldn't drift off to sleep until the wee hours of the morning. She feared she'd never sleep normally again, and her anxiety increased her inability to fall asleep. After nearly two months of being unable to sleep well at night and feeling exhausted and irritable during the day, Kelly went to her family doctor.

"I think you have a chronic form of insomnia that was initially triggered by the adjustment your body made to new time zones," her doctor suggested. "When you returned from Beijing and didn't readjust to this time zone right away, you became anxious and stressed over your sleeplessness. Your anxiety over not being able to sleep made it more difficult to fall asleep like you did before, and now it's become a self-perpetuating pattern."

"What can we do?" Kelly asked.

"Well, we can discuss some of your lifestyle habits and sleep routines. And we will do just that in a moment. But I'd also like to put you on a short-term **regimen** of a prescription sleep aid."

"A sleeping pill? Aren't they addictive?"

Kelly's doctor shook his head. "No, not the sleep aid I'm prescribing for you. It's called Ambien. And I'd only like you to use it five, maybe seven days."

Kelly peppered her practitioner with more questions, the most complicated of which was, "How does it work?" Kelly's doctor spent the next several minutes answering the young woman's questions.

Sleep Drugs and the Brain

While different types of sleeping pills affect the brain in different ways, in general, most sleeping pills induce sleep by quieting certain parts and actions of the brain. The barbiturates, benzodiazepines, and the newer imidazopyridines work essentially the same way. In his book *The Promise of Sleep*, Dr. William C. Dement describes their process using an illustration of brakes and levers.

Every brain, according to Dr. Dement, has a braking system that periodically restrains its nerve activity to keep the brain from working too hard for too long and burning out. Think about running a race. If you were running a marathon, you couldn't run your fastest during every minute of the race. Why? Because you'd quickly exhaust your energy and muscle strength and wouldn't be able to finish. You'd "burn out." To run long distances, you have to pace yourself. The brain is no different; it needs to pace itself to function properly.

To pace itself, the brain has a special braking system that serves a similar function. It keeps your brain's nerve cells, called neurons, from doing too much for too long. It helps them slow down, rest, and conserve energy to function for the long haul. To help pace nerve activity, something has to turn on the brake. That something is what Dr. Dement calls a lever.

Dr. Dement's brain lever, which turns on the brain's braking system, is called a GABA receptor. GABA receptors are chemicals, called neurotransmitters, that exist in the space between nerve cells found in the brain. Neurons in the brain don't actually touch each other. In order to communicate they need something to carry their messages from one nerve cell to the next. These chemicals, the neurotransmitters, carry the messages; they allow neurons to communicate with each other.

When the pacing lever is "off," the brake is off, and GABA receptors allow continuous, uninterrupted communication between nerve cells. Messages come and go as they please. When the lever is "on," it turns the braking mechanism on, and GABA receptors block certain nerve cell communications, causing a slowing of nerve activity. This slowing results in sleep.

The type of sleep drugs called barbiturates attach themselves to GABA receptors and work to slow communication between all neurons in the brain. Their effect on the brain is broad and more generalized than other drugs and can affect many body systems. That's

Common Over-the-Counter Sleep Aids

Over-the-counter drugs (OTCs) are those that can be sold without a prescription. Although they can be legally used without a doctor's supervision, they are still drugs that can cause side effects and should only be taken as directed. Some of the most common OTCs used to help a person sleep are:

Excedrin PM
Tylenol PM
Nytol
Sleep Eze
Sleepinal Night-Time Sleep Aid
Sominex
Unisom Nighttime Sleep Aid
Nyquil
Benadryl (an allergy medication)
melatonin (a natural sleep hormone)

why barbiturates not only induce sleep but also create addiction and can be lethal if overdosed.

Benzodiazepines work a little differently: they attach to a single, different part of the GABA receptor and only slow down communication between nerve cells that affect muscles and emotions. Rather than a widespread impact, these drugs result in muscle relaxation and reduced anxiety, which results in better sleep.

Ambien and other drugs of the newer class of hypnotics are even more selective in their approach; they attach themselves only to one small subpart of the receptor, which means their effect is even more targeted. A person taking Ambien will generally fall asleep quickly and suffer fewer side effects because the drug works on the lever in a very specific way.

In general, sleeping pills temporarily slow down communication between neurons in the brain. This slowing of communication ultimately results in sleep.

In Kelly's case, her brain's lever and braking system were working at the wrong time. Taking Ambien put the brake on at the right time (bedtime in New York's time zone), which enabled her brain to slow down enough to sleep when it was appropriate to sleep. After a few days on Ambien, her internal clock began to synchronize with her drug-induced sleep schedule, and by the end of a week, Kelly could sleep appropriately on her own. She no longer needed to take Ambien.

Drug Treatment: A Last Resort

As we have discovered, drug treatments for sleep disruptions have been around for centuries. From Morpheus, the Greek god of dreams, whose father Hypnos carried opium in his hands, to today's new safer class of hypnotics, sleep remedies have been the hope of sleep-plagued people throughout time. Some remedies were dangerous and addictive; others helped their patients' needs. But each successive treatment proved to be an advance in our battle for peaceful sleep.

With the progress we've made in our understanding of chemistry, biology, and the study of sleep, medications used to treat sleep disorders have improved greatly over the years. Because of these improvements, many safe, effective drugs are available today. Despite these advances, however, doctors still consider drug treatment *a last resort* in the battle against sleep disorders.

The reluctance to use drugs for sleep disturbances may seem surprising when popping a pill sounds like a quick, easy solution to troubled sleep. But sleep, as we learned in the first chapter of this book, is a complicated process of stages and timing, many parts of which can go wrong. Doctors often first examine other issues, like personal habits, sleep routines, and lifestyle choices, to determine if the patient's actions might cause or contribute to his sleep difficulties. Once those possibilities have been fully examined, and once other nondrug strategies have been tried and ruled out, doctors today can turn to newer prescription sleep aids as a safe, viable treatment option. But no drug treatment plan is without risks.

What we do during the day and before we go to bed can affect our sleep patterns.

Chapter Four

Sleep Disorder Treatment

When you experience problems with sleep that last for more than a few nights and your sleep problems are severe enough to disrupt your normal behavior, it's time to see a doctor. In order for your doctor to help your sleep problem, she has to uncover its cause.

Medical professionals and sleep researchers generally look for the root of your sleep trouble in any of four places: lifestyle choices or health habits, illness or health conditions, psychiatric problems, or sleep disorders.

Lifestyle Choices or Health Habits

The first areas a doctor will examine for causes for sleep troubles are your circumstances and daily habits. Has anything happened recently to cause you to worry? Are you under unusual stress? Do you eat sweets or drink caffeine-containing beverages after dinner or close to bedtime? Are you getting sufficient exercise? Do you go to bed at a regular time each night and get up at about the same time each morning? Do you drink alcohol, smoke cigarettes, or abuse drugs?

Stress, worry, eating habits, physical fitness, bedtime routines, and substance abuse—all of these can affect the way you sleep. Based on your description of your sleep troubles and answers you provide about your lifestyle, your doctor can determine if the source of your sleep problems is found here. If lifestyle choices or habits are the root of your sleep difficulty, your doctor will recommend appropriate steps you can take to develop a more sleep-friendly lifestyle. If lifestyle and habits are not the cause, she'll look for an underlying medical condition.

Health Conditions

On the first big snow of the season, twelve-year-old Daniel grabbed his sled and headed for the steep hill in his backyard. On his very first run, in a courageous attempt to "thread the needle" between two walnut trees, Dan lost control and plowed feet first into the left-hand trunk. He broke three bones in his foot.

That night, and for weeks afterward, Dan couldn't sleep. The walking cast the doctor put on his left foot was heavy and uncomfortable. He couldn't sleep on his stomach as he normally did, and he couldn't fall asleep on his back. If he stretched out on his side, his foot throbbed in pain.

When Dan's mother called the doctor about his sleep problems, the cause was clear: Daniel did not have a sleep disorder; his sleep

Smoking can interfere with your ability to sleep.

disturbance was due to the pain and discomfort caused by a broken limb. His physician quickly identified an existing health condition as the source of the adolescent's sleep disturbance.

Many medical conditions can create problems in sleep. Sometimes it's a painful injury (like Dan's broken foot), sometimes a disease (like juvenile arthritis, chronic bronchitis, or muscular dystrophy). If you have an ongoing medical condition that robs you of sleep, or if treatment for a chronic illness results in sleeplessness for you, your doctor needs to know. He may be able to change your current treatment plan or suggest ways to improve your sleep.

Psychiatric Problems

Underlying psychiatric problems such as depression, attention-deficit/hyperactivity disorder (ADHD), anxiety disorder, or bipolar disorder can also cause sleep disruptions. In his book on psychiatric drugs titled *Straight Talk about Psychiatric Medications for Kids*, Dr. Timothy Wilens mentions the case of a sixteen-year-old named Sam who has bipolar disorder.

bipolar disorder: A mood disorder characterized by periods of extreme highs and extreme lows.

manic: Period of extreme highs, including activity level.

Sam was able to recognize the start of his "high" period by a change in his sleep pattern. This teenager normally slept for about eight hours, but when the manic phase of his bipolar disorder kicked in, Sam only slept three or four hours per night.

Though his symptoms were similar to sleep disturbances such as delayed sleep phase syndrome (DSPS) and insomnia, Sam did not have a sleep disorder. He had an underlying psychiatric disorder that disturbed his sleep. In this case, Dr. Wilens treated Sam's primary problem, his bipolar disorder, which alleviated his sleep symptoms.

Developing a Sleep-Friendly Lifestyle

Try to go to bed at about the same time each night.
Establish a relaxing bedtime routine (warm bath, reading, etc.).
Maintain a healthy, balanced diet.
Exercise, but not too close to bedtime.
Don't nap during the day. If you must, limit your nap to fifteen or twenty minutes.
Make dinner your lightest meal.
Don't eat within three hours of bedtime.
If you crave a bedtime snack, make it a dairy protein (like milk or yogurt).
Get rid of caffeine.
Eliminate substance abuse (nicotine, alcohol, drugs).
Make your bedroom a work- and television-free zone.
Create a sleep-friendly environment to sleep in (dark, quiet room, comfortable bed).

Is It a Sleep Disorder?

If all other issues have been ruled out, your doctor may suspect a sleep disorder. If so, he might recommend that you visit a sleep clinic for additional testing. If experts at the sleep clinic determine that your sleep troubles are a diagnosable sleep disorder, don't expect them to put you on pills and send you on your way. Except in rare circumstances, long-term drug treatment is almost never prescribed for sleep disorders. Most treatment plans for sleep disorders include suggestions for lifestyle changes, improved habits, appropriate nondrug medical interventions (surgery to remove excess tissue in the throat, for example, in

sleep clinic: A medical facility that specializes in the diagnosis of sleep disorders.

Three Ways to Improve Your Sleep

According to Doctors Peter Hauri and Shirley Linde in their classic work on sleep disorders, *No More Sleepless Nights*, every person who has difficulty sleeping can do these three things to improve their sleep:

1. Reduce caffeine.
2. Limit alcohol.
3. Quit smoking.

cases of sleep apnea), and then, if necessary, short-term drug treatment.

That's what happened to the sleep-deprived college professor described in the following case study, which originally appeared in Dr. Dement's *The Promise of Sleep*. We'll call her Professor Pam and summarize (and adapt) her story here.

Teachers Have
Sleep Troubles, Too

Professor Pam went to see Dr. Dement because she hadn't been able to sleep for several weeks. The doctor's first step was to find out the exact nature of the sleep problem.

"How long has your sleep trouble been going on?" and "What does your pattern of sleep look like?" were two of the questions he asked during their first interview.

fibromyalgia: Chronic and frequent pain in the muscles and soft tissue surrounding the muscles.

Based on Professor Pam's answers, Dr. Dement suspected she might have a mild case of DSPS, but it didn't seem like it was serious enough to cause the symptoms she described.

How much caffeine are you *really* ingesting per day?

Caffeine is a drug that speeds up your body's processes, including the actions of your central nervous system. Yes, a little caffeine can help you feel more awake, but too much can give you headaches, make you feel agitated, give you "the shakes," and disrupt your sleep. Most people know that coffee contains caffeine, but many other food products also contain this stimulant. Here's a partial list of caffeine-containing foods and beverages.

coffee (5 oz. serving of drip-brewed)	115 mg. of caffeine
latté or cappucino (Starbucks, 8 oz.)	89 mg. of caffeine
decaffeinated coffee (5 oz.)	5 mg. of caffeine
Snapple iced tea (16-oz. bottle)	48 mg. of caffeine
regular or diet Coke (12 oz.)	46 mg. of caffeine
Jolt (12 oz.)	71 mg. of caffeine
Mountain Dew (12 oz.)	55 mg. of caffeine
chocolate milk (8 oz.)	5 mg. of caffeine
Hershey's milk chocolate (1.5 oz.)	10 mg. of caffeine
1/4 cup of semisweet chocolate chips	33 mg. of caffeine
one Hershey's chocolate kiss	1.2 mg. of caffeine
chocolate syrup (1 oz.)	4 mg. of caffeine
chocolate brownie (1 oz.)	6 mg. of caffeine

After asking several more questions, Dr. Dement ruled out other medical conditions (like fibromyalgia) and other sleep disorders (like restless leg syndrome). Existing medical conditions or psychological disorders weren't the cause. Could it be Professor Pam's lifestyle or habits? He knew she was health conscious, ate well, and exercised regularly. What could it be?

Dr. Dement questioned the young college professor about her stress level. Yes, she was under a lot of pressure at the college where she taught. Yes, she often worked late and worked right up until bedtime. Yes, she would lie awake at night worrying about her students or about a lecture she needed to give. Ah-ha! The source of her insomnia must be stress!

Dr. Dement suggested the following:

"Stay away from caffeine and alcohol, take a warm bath before bed, and when you turn out the lights and close your eyes, focus on a pleasant memory until you fall asleep. Don't think about school when you're going to sleep."

Professor Pam was eager to try Dr. Dement's suggestions and did so for the next several days. When she returned to see the doctor, she told him that she had tried everything he'd told her to do but that she still couldn't sleep.

The doctor's next plan was to eliminate his patient's worry about not being able to sleep. Sometimes worrying about whether or not you can sleep actually causes you to be unable to sleep.

"You need to set aside an early-evening 'worry time' to list your worries. Then list them! But once you've listed them, you're not allowed to think about them again for the rest of the evening, even at bedtime." Dr. Dement sent the professor home to try his "worry time" plan for two weeks.

When the two weeks were up, though she again had done what the doctor suggested, Professor Pam's symptoms still had not improved. It was time to send her to a sleep clinic.

Her sleep test results showed that Professor Pam really did have a sleep disorder. It was what Dr. Dement originally suspected, but it was worse than he thought. His patient's DSPS was more involved than he imagined.

Dr. Dement recommended that Professor Pam turn on bright lights in the morning to help her wake up earlier in the day, which would cause her to become sleepier in the evening. He also decided to put her on a low dosage of a sleeping pill for a week. He prescribed Ambien.

Going to a Sleep Clinic?

If your doctor recommends that you be tested at a sleep clinic, here's what you can expect:

- The clinic staff will ask you to complete a lengthy questionnaire.
- Your first appointment and interview will last approximately two hours.
- You will probably have a complete physical and neurological exam.
- The clinic staff may want you to come back and stay overnight to monitor your sleep.

If the staff decides you need an overnight appointment, you can expect the following once you check in for your one-night stay:

- You will change into pajamas or a sleeping gown (usually your own).
- Wires will be painlessly attached to your head, chest, and legs.
- You may have a tube hooked up to your throat to measure air pressure.
- You will sleep alone in a darkened room.
- Clinic staff will monitor your sleep throughout the night from a nearby room, usually by watching machines and computers that record data from the sensors that were attached to you when you arrived.
- You will sleep through the night at the clinic.
- In the morning, a specialist will analyze your data and make suggestions to you and your doctor about how to improve your sleep. Then you can go home.

"I know you're hesitant about taking a sleeping pill," Dr. Dement said, "but I'd like you to try taking a small dose of Ambien for a week."

"What's Ambien?" the professor asked suspiciously.

"Ambien is a newer, fast-acting sleep aid that has very few side effects. Its chemical name is zolpidem tartrate, though most people know it by its trade name, Ambien. Zolpidem has become today's drug of choice for treating short-term insomnia because, unlike the old sleeping pills, it's safe and not addictive. It's also easy to take—just a single dose right before bedtime."

"If I agree to try Ambien, how much do I have to take?"

"We'll start you out on only five milligrams. That should do it, although you can take up to as much as twenty. I'll write a script for just seven of the five-milligram tabs, and we can see how it goes. Let's just try it for one week. What do you think?"

Professor Pam thought for a moment. "Are the pills difficult to swallow?"

"Not at all," her doctor assured. "The five-milligram tabs come as a small, pink, capsule-shaped tablet with a film coating to make it easier to go down."

Still hesitant about taking a sleeping pill, the young professor pressed Dr. Dement for more information.

"Will this make me really tired when I get up? I mean, will it be in my system for a long time?"

Dr. Dement shook his head. "Ambien's half-life is very short. In as little as ninety minutes to four-and-a-half hours after taking it, nearly half of the drug will be out of your system. It will be completely gone in anywhere from three to nine hours. When Ambien is taken at bedtime, most people wake up feeling rested and ready to go."

"I don't know." The young professor hesitated. "How long does it take to work?"

"Ambien has been shown to help individuals fall asleep in as little as fifteen minutes. For some people it takes thirty, but rarely longer than that. You'll fall asleep pretty quickly."

Professor Pam still wasn't convinced.

"I've heard that some sleep aids mess up your normal sleep stages. Will Ambien do that to me?"

Dr. Dement shook his head again. "One of the reasons Ambien works so well is that is doesn't disrupt sleep stages. People who take Ambien still cycle through all four stages of non-REM sleep and the REM sleep stage throughout the night. Ambien will not harm your sleep architecture in any way. You don't need to worry about that."

"Sounds pretty safe." Professor Pam was warming to the idea. "Are there any risks I should know about?"

Dr. Dement thought for a moment. "As with any sleep aid, you should take it only when you're ready for bed. Never try to drive once you've taken it. Oh, and you must avoid alcohol completely while you're on it. In extreme cases, mixing Ambien with alcohol can affect your breathing."

"I'm not a drinker anyway."

The doctor paused, and then added, "As with any drug, there are slight risks of adverse reactions. The most common side effects are things like headache, fatigue, and nausea, but these happen in less than 10 percent of all cases. It's actually more like one percent. Side effects with this drug are pretty rare."

"Okay. I'm sold. Let's give it a go, but only for a week."

The doctor wasn't quite finished. "I want you to call me every morning to let me know how things have gone the night before. That way we'll know whether or not to increase your dosage."

"You got it, doc. I'll call you in the morning."

The combination of using bright lights in the morning and using a low dosage of sleep medication did the trick for Professor Pam. She felt much more rested during the day and didn't fear going to bed at night. After a one-week trial on Ambien,

half-life: The time necessary for the body, tissue, or organ to metabolize half the amount of a substance.

Alcohol and sleeping medication can be a deadly combination.

she was very relieved. Dr. Dement weaned Professor Pam off Ambien over a second week (having her take it every other day), until she was off it completely. She continued to sleep well after that.

Professor Pam's case illustrates how a treatment plan for sleep disorders includes several approaches. Dr. Dement gave the professor specific tasks to try to help reduce her stress. He encouraged her to change her bedtime routine to include relaxation techniques and a warm bath. He used bright light therapy and medications.

He also used several different methods of diagnosis. He ruled out other medical conditions; he talked with the young professor about her lifestyle, habits, and stress. He sent her to a sleep clinic. He used trial and error in treatment approaches to see what worked.

Treatment plans for most sleep disorders will use all of these things. And those that include drug treatment will often follow the same course as the plan Dr. Dement used with Professor Pam: a short-term trial on a low dosage of sleep medicine. Dr. Dement and Professor Pam provide just one illustration of how someone with a sleep disorder can be helped.

Lack of sleep can make people act grouchy, depressed—or silly.

Chapter Five

Case Studies in Sleep Disorders

Eleven-year-old Samantha thinks she might be going crazy. Over the past several months she's awakened to find herself in the wrong bed or wrong room. One night, after going to sleep in her own bedroom, she woke up frightened because she didn't know where she was. After a moment of confusion, she realized she was not in her bed but on the living room sofa downstairs. She didn't know how she got there. Other times she found herself in her younger sister's bed or on the floor of her brother's room without remembering going from her room to theirs.

Sleepy Teens

If you're a teen who wrestles with daytime sleepiness, you're not alone. According to a 2006 study conducted by the National Sleep Foundation, over half of America's teenagers complain of being tired during the day. More than a quarter have fallen asleep in school, while another 22 percent have fallen asleep doing homework.

Her little sister reports that she has seen Samantha walking around in the middle of the night, but Samantha never answers when she tries to talk to her. She says Samantha looks like a "zombie." Most nights, after strolling through the house, Samantha makes it back to her own bed, but sometimes she ends up in different rooms. These nights frightened her most.

Samantha can't remember leaving her room or walking around at night. She can't remember her sister trying to talk to her. She can't remember anything at all about her nighttime escapades except that she goes to sleep in her own bed and wakes up somewhere else. Her inability to remember scares Samantha as much as waking in strange places. Is she going crazy?

Sixteen-year-old Jordan is frightened, too, but for a different reason. He can't stay awake during the day, no matter how hard he tries. He falls asleep in school. He falls asleep at the dinner table. He sometimes falls asleep on the bus ride home and misses his stop. Jordan doesn't even go out with friends anymore because he's afraid he'll make a fool of himself and fall asleep. Every day for the last three months he's had several "sleep attacks" during which he feels an irresistible urge to sleep.

Jordan thinks that his terrifying dreams are what make him so sleepy during the day. At night when he first goes to sleep or in the morning just before he awakes, he sometimes thinks someone is standing over him, threatening him somehow. He wakes up literally

Are You Sleep Deprived?

The National Sleep Foundation's publication *Adolescent Sleep Needs and Patterns* lists four signs of sleep deprivation in youth under age eighteen. Do any of these describe you or someone you know?

1. Difficulty waking in the morning.
2. Irritability late in the day.
3. Falling asleep spontaneously during quiet times of the day.
4. Sleeping for extra long periods on the weekends.

If so, you (or your friend) may be dangerously sleep deprived.

---

paralyzed with fear. Unable to move or scream, Jordan lies there until the feeling passes. It's getting so that he's afraid to fall asleep at night. But his dreams aren't what frighten Jordan most.

When Jordan gets really upset, his body goes limp and he can't move. Jordan is terrified that he's developing a strange disease, or worse yet, that he might be having "seizures" like his cousin Jeremy has. Is Jordan as sick as he fears he is?

High school junior Carrie used to be an active, achieving student. At the top of her class, Carrie handled her advanced-placement courses with ease. She participated in several after-school activities, but she most enjoyed her role as cocaptain of her field hockey team. In addition to her studies and extracurricular activities, Carrie worked part-time at a local convalescent home where senior citizens there described her as "always cheerful" and "a pleasure to have around." Everything in Carrie's life seemed to be going well . . . until a few weeks ago.

People who don't get enough sleep are often irritable and easily provoked.

Over the last month and a half, Carrie hasn't been able to get to sleep before three or four o'clock in the morning. Falling asleep so late when she has to get up by six a.m. for school is wearing out Carrie. She's so tired she can hardly think straight. She's become grumpy and irritable with people at work. Her friends think she's "checking out," because she doesn't seem to listen to their problems as well as she used to. And because she can't get the sleep she needs on school nights, Carrie sleeps late on weekends, sometimes as late as two or three in the afternoon, which cuts into her study time and social life. Carrie's grades, friendships, and job performance are starting to suffer. What's wrong?

Carrie, Jordan, and Samantha aren't sick, at least not in the usual sense. They don't have life-threatening diseases or illnesses. They don't have emotional problems. Though they are different ages and face different challenges, all three are ordinary young people who happen to struggle with sleep disorders: Carrie has delayed sleep phase syndrome; Jordan is experiencing narcolepsy; Samantha wrestles with sleepwalking disorder. Can anything be done for them?

Help for Samantha's Sleepwalking

We learned in earlier chapters that sleepwalking usually occurs during the deeper stages of sleep: Stages Three and Four. We also learned that sleepwalking often begins in childhood and peaks during the preteen years. At eleven, Samantha is at the age where she is most likely to sleepwalk.

As long as Samantha's sleepwalking isn't causing injury to herself or others, and as long as she's not leaving the house during her nighttime strolls, Samantha's doctor would likely take a nondrug-treatment approach with a wait-and-see attitude. Samantha can expect her sleepwalking episodes to disappear on their own by the time she reaches age fifteen, perhaps even before. In the meantime, her doctor might tell Samantha to do the following:

- Go to the bathroom immediately before going to bed (a full bladder sometimes triggers sleepwalking episodes).
- Avoid drinking anything before bedtime.
- Establish a calming bedtime routine (take a hot bath, listen to quiet music, read a book, etc.).
- Make sure to get enough rest (excessive tiredness can cause more sleepwalking).
- Remove any sharp or dangerous objects from her room.
- If possible, switch to a ground floor bedroom (to reduce the risk of falling down stairs).
- Before going to bed, close and lock exterior doors and windows.

If, however, Samantha's sleepwalking becomes dangerous (she falls down steps or runs out of the house) or if she sleepwalks every night or several times a night and can't get the rest she needs, her doctor

Soothing bedtime routines can help a person get to sleep—but drinking anything at bedtime can contribute to sleepwalking.

might prescribe a short-term regimen on a low dosage of a benzo-diazepine (the class of drugs that suppresses Stages Three and Four of the sleep cycle).

Though medication is not usually recommended for treating children with sleepwalking disorder, when symptoms are severe enough, a small dose of diazepam (Valium) or lorazepam (Ativan) has been known to bring relief.

Samantha isn't crazy and she need not fear. She can find help for her midnight meanders.

Good News for Jordan's Narcolepsy

Unlike Samantha, Jordan's symptoms, including his excessive day-time sleepiness (EDS), cataplexy, and sleep paralysis, are not something he will outgrow. Narcolepsy is a chronic, lifelong condition that often first appears during the teen years. Though this sleep disorder cannot be "cured," it can be treated. That's good news.

chronic: Frequent or long term.

When Jordan discussed his symptoms with his family physician, the doctor immediately suspected narcolepsy. Narcolepsy, if you recall, is a condition in which a person experiences sudden, uncontrollable attacks of REM sleep, skipping the normal sleep stages and jumping almost immediately to the dream stage. These sleep attacks can happen anyplace at any-time, which explains Jordan's falling-asleep episodes at school, on the bus, and at the dinner table. Jordan's doctor suggested that Jordan go to a sleep treatment center to be evaluated. Testing done at the sleep center will prove or disprove the doctor's suspicions.

When he arrived for his sleep test, Jordan was hooked up to a polysomnograph to measure his sleep patterns. He would be tested both at night and during the day. While observing Jordan's sleep, the clinic specialist discovered that even during daytime hours Jordan fell asleep in less than ten minutes and that both at night and during the day he almost immediately entered REM sleep (skipping the usual first four stages of NREM sleep). Jordan's experience at the sleep center confirmed his doctor's suspicions: Jordan had narcolepsy.

The goal of treatment for narcolepsy is to treat the symptoms since the disorder itself cannot be cured. One of the most troubling symptoms for Jordan was his EDS: the excessive daytime sleepiness that made him suffer "sleep attacks." To treat EDS, doctors often prescribe a class of drugs called stimulants. These drugs speed up the body's processes and help the patient stay alert. Stimulants, however, can have unwanted side effects: dizziness, irritability, loss of appetite, and sleep disruption (when you want to sleep).

A new drug called modafinil (Provigil) works differently than the stimulants and causes fewer side effects. It was the first drug specifically developed for the treatment of EDS and narcolepsy in more than forty years and was approved by the FDA for use in the United States in 1998. It became available by prescription in 1999. This "wake-up" pill can help a person feel more awake without causing problems that other narcolepsy medications commonly cause. Most important, it is not addictive and does not disrupt nighttime sleep. In 2007, a similar drug called Nuvigil (armodafinil) was also released, offering patients with narcolepsy another option.

When Jordan's doctor received the results of Jordan's sleep clinic tests, she put the sixteen-year-old on two hundred milligrams of modafinil, to be taken once a day in the morning. In addition to medication, Jordan's doctor suggested that he schedule two ten- to fifteen-minute naps during the day to control his daytime sleepiness. She also encouraged Jordan to get plenty of regular daytime exercise, to avoid caffeine and alcohol, and to get sufficient sleep at night. The more Jordan took control over his sleep habits, the more successful he would be in alleviating his EDS.

Provigil can help a person with narcolepsy feel more awake without unwanted side effects.

Regular exercise routines can help prevent excessive daytime sleepiness.

The combination of medication and lifestyle changes, along with the encouragement of a teen narcolepsy support group that Jordan joined, helped Jordan figure out how to live with his condition. His sleep disorder wasn't cured, but Jordan learned to successfully manage his symptoms and live a relatively normal life.

Dealing with Carrie's Delayed Sleep Phase Syndrome

Carrie doesn't have the same treatment options available to her that Samantha and Jordan have. Unfortunately for this exhausted high school student, her sleep difficulties stem from a problem with her internal biological clock. For the long term, sleep drugs won't help her. But that doesn't mean that Carrie can't find help. She can try several alternative treatments. We will take a closer look at alternate and supplementary treatment strategies for sleep disorders in chapter 7, but we can mention some of the strategies here that Carrie found most helpful.

When Carrie discussed her sleep problems with her doctor, he explained that Carrie's internal clock was off. Her body was telling her to stay awake when it was time to sleep and to sleep when it was time to wake. The bad news was that no matter what she did, she wouldn't be able to back up the clock.

As author Linda Bayer noted in *Sleep Disorders*, dealing with a delayed sleep clock is like driving down a one-way street. Assume that an appropriate bedtime is located at a house halfway down the block. With a delayed sleep clock, your body drives past the house, and you can't back up to get there again. The only solution, then, is to drive the entire way around the block until you reach the house once more. This is what Carrie had to do.

The key to Carrie's overcoming her delayed sleep problem was to "trick" her internal clock into running with normal sleeping/waking hours. The only way she could do that was to drive all the way "around the block" again. Practically speaking, this meant that Carrie had to delay her bedtime by an hour every day until she made it all the way around the clock to a normal time for bed.

On Monday, Carrie's delayed clock wouldn't let her fall asleep until four a.m., so that's when she went to bed. The next night, Tuesday, she forced herself to stay up an hour later, until five a.m. On Wednesday, she pushed her bedtime back another hour to six a.m. On Thursday she waited until seven a.m. Carrie continued this one-hour delay over the next two weeks (going to bed successively later through the morning, afternoon, and evening) until her bedtime came back around to eleven p.m. Then she stopped delaying her bedtime and continued going to bed at that time. Throughout the process, for every hour she delayed her bedtime, she also got up one

Worries can keep a person awake!

hour later than the previous day, maintaining an eight-hour sleep every night. When Carrie established her final bedtime at eleven p.m., she also made her wake-up time seven a.m. After several weeks of sleep change, which required much patience and diligence, Carrie was back on a normal sleep schedule.

The fancy term for this "driving around the block" to change an internal clock is chronotherapy. This nondrug treatment is only one of several alternative treatments (see chapter seven).

Although they suffered with different sleep disorders and pursued different treatment strategies, Samantha, Jordan, and Carrie each found help. The key for all three was that they sought professional assistance.

If you ever have problems sleeping, medical professionals can assess your sleep difficulty and determine the best course of action for you. Depending on the diagnosis, drug treatment may or may not be part of their treatment plan. If it is, make sure to ask about potential risks and side effects of any drug therapy your doctor recommends.

When sleep won't come, many people turn to a sleeping aid. These medications, however, can have unwanted side effects.

Chapter Six

The Risks of Sleep Disorder Treatment

On a Thursday night in December, Janelle wanted to finish working on Christmas cards she'd made so she could take them with her to school the next morning. Friday was the last day of school before break, and the high school freshman knew she wouldn't see many of her classmates and friends until January. Finishing her greetings now would save her the cost of postage—and besides, she liked playing Santa in person.

Janelle's intentions were good, but she'd also just taken a sleep aid her doctor prescribed for her when she saw him that morning. *Surely I can finish these last two cards,* the teenager thought as she continued working. *I know he told me not take my medicine until I was in bed, but it's only one little pill. A few minutes won't hurt.*

Twenty minutes later, she couldn't hold her pen. She glanced up from her work toward the cellar door. The doorknob appeared to be melting. *What's happening to me?*

Janelle tried to stand up but felt too weak and dizzy to do so. Getting down onto her hands and knees, she crawled out to the stairwell and called up to her father.

"Daddy, I can't get up! Daddy, please help me!"

Thankfully, Janelle's experience was only a passing, short-lived reaction to the mild sleep aid she'd taken. Her father carried his daughter to her room, where she quickly fell asleep and slept soundly through the night. In the morning, she was fine.

For some people, though, their reactions aren't so fine.

In our medicine-prone culture, we often don't think about the risks involved in popping a pill. Got a headache? Take an aspirin. Sneezing too much? Take an allergy pill. You name the problem, there's probably a pill to treat it. The same goes for sleep troubles.

The Complete Idiot's Guide to Getting a Good Night's Sleep reports that more than thirteen million people in the United States take some kind of prescribed drug to help them sleep. In his book *Overcoming Insomnia,* Dr. Donald Sweeney notes that doctors write between twenty and thirty million prescriptions for sleep aids and tranquilizers per year. What many patients fail to realize is that sleeping pills (and other sleep aid drugs), especially when used for longer periods of time, have a downside: they cause unintended responses in our bodies. These side effects, called adverse reactions, can happen to anyone as a result of any drug.

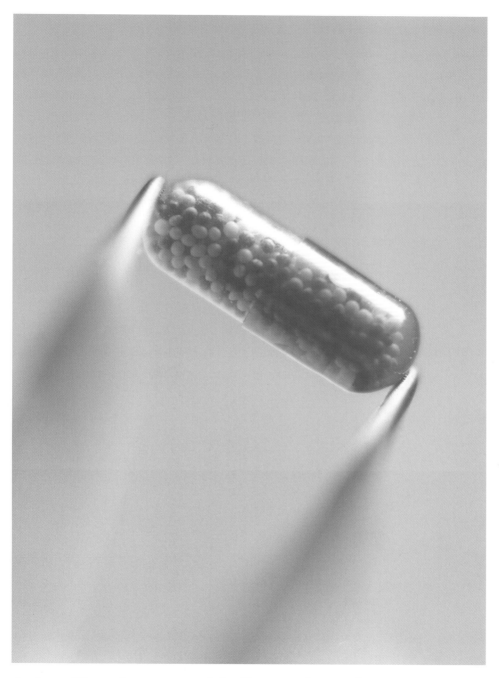

A tiny pill can have powerful effects on brain chemistry, altering normal sleep architecture.

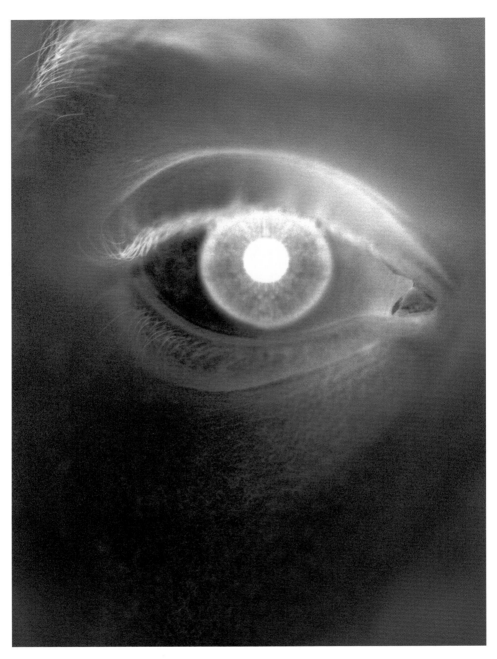

Wakefulness can be caused by a number of medical conditions. Sleep aids can help you get your eyes shut—but they may hide the real cause of your problem.

Risk/Side Effect #1
Sleep Drugs Alter
Your Sleep Architecture

Yes, changing the pattern of your sleep is exactly what sleep medications are supposed to do. The danger comes when you take a sleep drug for more than just a few days. These medications can make your body skip certain sleep stages, and when you don't get enough sleep in all sleep stages, your brain and body just don't have the chance to recover the way they do when you experience every stage of sleep.

Drugs for sleep problems should almost always be a short-term *temporary* solution. The longer you take a sleep drug, the more likely you are to have problems with your cycles of sleep.

Risk/Side Effect #2
Sleeping Pills Can Mask
Other Medical Problems

Thirteen-year-old Tommy couldn't sleep. He'd been having trouble sleeping since Bear, his Labrador retriever, died seven months ago. Bear had been his best buddy for as long as Tommy could remember. They grew up together, and now he was gone.

To sleep better at night, Tommy took some Tylenol PM® out of his parents' bathroom's medicine cabinet. (Never do this!) He took two tablets, and it worked—he slept soundly. But for the next several weeks, though he was sleeping at night, Tommy felt irritable and lethargic almost every day. He realized that the chronic tiredness he had thought was caused by not sleeping must be caused by something else.

The Problem with Sleeping Pills

Although today's generation of sleeping pills can provide safe, effective help for short-term sleep disturbances, they aren't perfect. Here are some of their dangers:

- Sleeping pills affect people differently. You may not be able to predict how it will work in you.
- A sleeping pill's effects can last not only through the night but into the next day.
- Drowsiness from sleeping pills can cause accidents.
- Sleeping pills can be addictive.
- Sleeping pills can be habit-forming.
- Sleeping pills can cause further sleep problems.
- Sleeping pills can hide other medical problems.
- Sleeping pills are a short-term fix.
- Sleeping pills can cause dangerous side effects.
- Sleeping pills can interact with other drugs in harmful ways.
- Sleeping pills plus alcohol can equal death.

Tommy was right. It was something else. Tommy was depressed. One of the classic symptoms of depression is inability to sleep. By taking an over-the-counter sleep aid and not telling anyone about his symptoms, Tommy kept himself and everyone around him from discovering the true cause of his irritability and fatigue.

Taking sleep aids can help improve sleep, but they can also hide underlying problems that may be causing the sleeplessness. Inability to sleep is a symptom of many medical conditions, some serious, which is why you should always see your doctor before you start taking drugs to help you sleep. He can test you for any medical conditions that might disturb your sleep.

Risk/Side Effect #3
Sleep Aids May Become
Addictive or Habit-Forming

Do you drink colas or coffee regularly? Have you ever tried to quit drinking these caffeine-laced beverages? If so, you probably experienced headaches or became irritable. Why? When your body gets used to having a regular influx of caffeine (or any other drug substance), it becomes dependent on it. You're hooked. And when you take caffeine (or other drugs) away, your body goes through a process of withdrawal. Headaches and irritability are signs of this.

The same process happens with cocaine, alcohol, and nicotine. It happens with many sleeping pills, too. Your body becomes used to the drugs, just as it would any other addictive substance, and then it craves them. You're addicted.

Physical addiction was a huge problem for older drug classes, especially barbiturates. Today's sleep aids, though not addictive, tend to be habit-forming instead. What's the difference? Being addicted to a drug means we physically need the drug, and if we don't get it, we suffer physical consequences (like headaches in caffeine withdrawal, or tremors during alcohol withdrawal). If a drug is only habit-forming (not truly addictive), it means we learn to psychologically depend on the drug (it becomes a habit), even though our physical bodies don't need or crave it.

If a sleep drug becomes a habit for us, when we try to stop taking it, we may find that we have more trouble sleeping than we did before we took the drug. This process results in even greater difficulties with sleep.

Risk/Side Effect #4
Sleep Drugs Can Cause
Additional Sleep Troubles

One characteristic of sleep aids is that they become less effective the longer we use them. To continue getting the same effect from a sleeping pill, we need to take higher and higher doses over time. And with every higher dose, we become more dependent. When we try to stop taking the sleep drugs on which we've learned to depend, our sleepless nights return.

In his book *The Essential Guide to Psychiatric Drugs*, Dr. Jack Gorman describes the process this way:

> A person can't fall asleep for a few nights for whatever reason. So she buys over-the-counter sleeping pills or takes some Valium from the medicine cabinet. She sleeps fine for a week. Then the effect starts wearing off, so she takes a second sleeping pill in the middle of the night when she wakes up. Soon, her body becomes trained to expect a middle-of-the-night sleeping pill and she automatically wakes up for it. Before long, she awakens regularly several times through the night. She tells the doctor that she can't sleep, "even though I am taking sleeping pills." The real danger here is that the patient and doctor become misled into thinking that the insomnia is so bad it is breaking through the sleeping pills, and they conclude incorrectly that stronger sleeping pills are needed. In fact, sleeping pills often disrupt normal sleep cycle and therefore cause insomnia.

For the woman described above, taking sleeping pills only made her problem worse. She experienced a side effect called "rebound insomnia." This effect can last for several weeks. Though unpleasant to live with, rebound insomnia isn't a permanent condition and will pass with time. Sadly, the same cannot be said for all adverse reactions.

Risk/Side Effect #5
Sleep Aids May Cause
Adverse Reactions

Sleep drugs of every kind (prescription and nonprescription alike) can cause unexpected side effects. That's why it's important to never take a drug without first talking with your doctor. Some of the most common reactions that result from sleep drugs include:

- sleepiness during the day
- memory trouble
- dizziness
- upset stomach
- muscle weakness
- slowed reactions
- confusion
- hallucinations

As scary as these may be, some of the most dangerous side effects have to do with how the drug affects you the next day. What might happen if you are groggy while you try to operate farm machinery or power tools? What if you get behind the wheel of a car? Remember Michael Doucette's automobile accident? If taking a sleep aid at night makes you unable to be alert during the day, you might seriously hurt yourself or someone else. And those injuries may be permanent.

If you experience any unexpected symptoms after you start taking a sleep drug, even if it's only daytime drowsiness, call your physician. He may lower your dose or take you off the drug completely. Or he may be able to prescribe a different drug with fewer side effects.

Risk/Side Effect #6
Possible Lethal Overdoses or Interactions with Other Drugs

Sleeping pills first got their bad reputation in the 1950s and 1960s when several celebrities combined these drugs with alcohol in deadly suicides. The most famous of these was Marilyn Monroe. The famous Hollywood actress, known for her sex appeal, blonde hair, windblown skirts, and vulnerability, was found dead on August 5, 1962. The cause of her death? An overdose of the sleeping pill Nembutal (a popular barbiturate) probably combined with alcohol. Though historians still debate whether her death was an accidental overdose, suicide, or conspiracy-born murder, the role drugs and alcohol played in her death remains unchallenged.

Most modern classes of sleep drugs don't hold the deadly overdose potential that the earlier sleep drugs like Nembutal held, but even today's drugs can have dangerous consequences if mixed with other drugs, alcohol, or abused substances.

Ambien, one of the safest and most effective sleeping pills available, can be extremely dangerous if combined with alcohol: it can cause you to stop breathing. One rule to follow with any sleep drug is to never drink alcohol while you're taking the medication. The choice to drink and take sleeping pills, no matter how "safe" they seem, could kill you.

If you need to take a drug to help you sleep, always, always, always be sure to tell your doctor about any other medications, herbs, or vitamins you are taking. This information could save your life.

Janelle's experience at the start of this chapter is a more typical experience of side effects. Her reaction was short term and not life threatening. It passed with time. But it was serious. Her hallucination (the doorknob melting) and inability to stand are stark reminders that sleep drugs are strong drugs that affect the mind and body in ways we don't entirely understand.

What should I do if I have an adverse reaction?

- If you're a minor, tell your parents.
- Call (or have your parents call) your doctor immediately.
- Report every detail of your reaction, no matter how small.
- Tell the doctor if you took other drugs or alcohol while taking this medication.
- If the reaction is affecting your ability to breathe, get to a hospital.
- Don't abruptly stop taking a drug unless your doctor tells you to do so.

Knowing that powerful drugs come with powerful risks, some people prefer to try different treatment strategies to help their sleep problems—treatments that don't include medications.

Restless leg syndrome can make you feel wide awake.

Chapter Seven

Alternative and Supplementary Treatments

Kevin couldn't lie still. The awful "creepy crawly" feeling in his legs just wouldn't go away. His feet itched. Then it felt like soda pop was bubbling in his veins. Next both legs felt prickly.

He tried rubbing his feet together. He tried wiggling them. He tried kicking, stretching, and shaking his legs under the covers. It was no use. He'd never get any sleep. As long as Kevin rested the sensation grew worse; it always did, especially at night. If he got up and walked around, he found some relief. Tossing aside his comforter and sheet, the thirteen-year-old rolled out of bed.

Lavender is a natural remedy that can help promote sleep.

No sleep tonight, Kevin sighed. *Another pooped day tomorrow.*

Kevin is experiencing the classic symptoms of restless legs syndrome (RLS). Although there are several drugs used to treat RLS, the FDA has only approved two—ropinirole (Requip) and pramipexole (Mirapex). Kevin may not find help in prescription drugs, but RLS is a sleep disorder where alternatives to drugs are often used.

Common Alternatives: Vitamins, Minerals, and Herbs

For RLS patients, one common alternative to prescription drug therapy is the use of vitamin supplements. Some experts suggest that RLS may be caused by shortages of iron, vitamin B_{12}, and folate in the body. Some RLS sufferers hoping to find relief take supplements containing these substances in an attempt to boost their vitamin and mineral levels.

RLS isn't the only sleep disorder people use supplements to treat. It's long been known that certain vitamins and minerals in your body can affect how long and how well you sleep; they directly affect your sleep architecture. Those substances most often said to impact sleep include calcium, magnesium, copper, iron, zinc, and several of the B vitamins: vitamin B_3 (niacin), folic acid, and vitamins B_5, B_6, and B_{12}. Many people with insomnia try taking these vitamins to help them fall asleep faster and stay asleep longer.

People have found the same result using herbs. Several herbs can help you relax, and they come in many forms. Chamomile, a well-known herbal remedy for sleep and headaches, is brewed as a tea. Another herb, hops, comes not only as dried tea like chamomile but in capsule form. It also comes as liquid in a medicine-dropper bottle. You can squeeze a few drops of hops underneath your tongue to be absorbed directly into your system, or you can put several drops in hot water to drink. Passionflower, another herb, can calm your nerves. It works much like a mild sedative. It's most often taken in

Being the only one awake can be a lonely feeling. Diet, lifestyle changes, and natural remedies may offer help.

capsule form. The common herb lavender, also used to treat insomnia, most often comes as an oil or tea.

Although herbs and vitamins can be helpful in treating some sleep disorders, it's important to remember that the FDA doesn't oversee the manufacture and sale of these supplements the same way it does prescription and over-the-counter drugs. Because the FDA doesn't control how dietary supplements are made, the amount of a certain vitamin, herb, or mineral found in one manufacturer's pill can differ from what you find in another. A calcium tablet made by Company A, for example, might contain five hundred milligrams of calcium. Company B's tablet may contain one thousand milligrams. Both tablets are calcium supplements, but one is twice as strong as the other. Because of the differences in tablet strength for unregulated drugs (including vitamins, herbs, and minerals), it can be easy to take too much.

Try Six L's to Get Some Zzz's

LEAVE your sleepless lifestyle behind! Realize that excessive tiredness can hurt your relationships and your ability to function at school, work, and sports. Make sleep a priority!

LAY OUT a consistent sleep schedule. Go to bed at roughly the same time each night; wake at the same time each morning. When that's not possible, try to stay within your routine by an hour or two.

LEARN how much sleep you need. Sleep needs vary, but researchers estimate that most young adults need eight-and-a-half to nine-and-a-quarter hours of sleep per night. What amount of sleep allows you to wake refreshed?

LIGHTEN UP. In other words, get into bright light as soon as possible after waking. But avoid bright light close to bedtime.

LIMIT substances that disrupt sleep, especially caffeine in sodas, chocolate, and coffee. Avoid alcohol and nicotine, which can also disturb sleep.

LOUNGE at bedtime. Help yourself relax by reading, taking a hot bath or listening to quiet music. Plan to fall asleep in bed (not on the couch while watching TV).

Another issue to remember is that just as prescription medications can cause unexpected reactions in your body, vitamins and herbs can also have side effects. Too much vitamin B_6, for example, can cause your hands and feet to feel clumsy and your mouth to feel numb. Just because it's a vitamin or herb doesn't mean it can't hurt you.

People who are uncomfortable taking dietary supplements sometimes look for a more "natural" way to help their sleep disturbances.

When to Halt Hormones

You should NOT take melatonin if you . . .
- are or might be pregnant.
- have diabetes, leukemia, or kidney disease.
- have a seizure disorder.
- suffer from migraine headaches.
- take steroids or steroidal medications.

What better alternative could they find than substances already produced in the body? Of the natural sleep disturbance treatments, the most common is melatonin.

The Hormone
of the Night

hormone: A substance originating in the body that is spread throughout the body, chemically stimulating specific parts to increase or decrease an activity.

Did you know that your body has a chemical response to light and darkness? When you snuggle into bed and turn out the lights, a structure in the base of your brain releases a hormone called melatonin. Your body produces this chemical primarily when it's dark. During the day, when you're awake and surrounded by light, your brain nearly stops producing this hormone, and melatonin levels go down. As the sun sets and your world darkens, your melatonin production begins again, and its levels rise. Melatonin levels are highest in the middle of the night.

Sleep researchers suggest that melatonin plays a part in making your internal clock work properly. When the dark outside causes

Massage can promote relaxation.

Do you feel happier on sunny days? Many people do—and it turns out that sunshine actually does have a biological effect on our emotions and brain chemistry. Our internal clocks are "set" by the patterns of light and dark around us. People who live in regions where there is little sunlight for long periods of time may feel sadder and sleepier. This is because the lack of light triggers their brains to produce more melatonin, a chemical that acts like a light switch inside our minds, telling us when to feel sleepy and when to feel alert.

your melatonin levels to increase, your brain begins the process of preparing the body for sleep. With the coming of dawn and daylight hours, your melatonin levels drop, and your brain awakes.

People with delayed sleep clocks, jet lag, or insomnia often take melatonin, hoping it will fix their sleep timing or help them fall asleep. This strategy yields mixed results. Some people claim that the hormone helps; others see no effect at all. Still others insist that melatonin makes it harder for them to get up in the morning and makes them sleepy all day.

Why do people react differently? The varying effects of melatonin may be due in part to the differences in how much hormone is found in a single dose. Melatonin comes in capsules, tablets, and liquid form, and the amount per dose varies with each manufacturer. Some products provide a one-milligram dose; others provide three milligrams. Most doctors and sleep experts suggest that you don't need any more than one-third to a half of a milligram to help you sleep. That means that most tablets sold in stores today are three to ten times stronger than the recommended dosage!

As with vitamins, the FDA does not oversee the making of this hormone supplement. You may not know how much melatonin you're getting in each pill. If you decide to take melatonin, be careful not to take too much. Hormone supplements (no matter how "natural" they claim to be) are strong chemicals that can cause side effects. Too much melatonin can backfire, making you too agitated or anxious to sleep.

seasonal depression: A mood disorder in which there is a connection between onset or disappearance of an episode and a particular time.

When taken at the right dosages, a melatonin supplement can be a safe alternative to drug therapy for raising melatonin levels and improving sleep. And if you're uncomfortable with taking a melatonin supplement, you can get melatonin by eating melatonin-contain-

Midnight Munchies to Help You Sleep

Authors Dr. Joyce Walsleben and Rita Baron-Faust recommend these sleep-inducing recipes in their book, *A Woman's Guide to Sleep: Guaranteed Solutions for a Good Night's Rest* (New York: Crown Publishers, 2000):

NIGHTLY NEWS MUNCH:
- 4–5 whole grain crackers
- 1–2 oz. sliced turkey, cheese, or tuna salad
- 8 oz. of nonfat or one percent milk

BREAKFAST AT BEDTIME:
- 1 sliced banana
- 1 cup high-fiber cold cereal
- 6 oz. nonfat or one percent milk
- (Optional: 1 tsp. ground soy nuts)

SLEEPER SMOOTHIE:
- Blend until smooth in electric blender:
- 1 sliced banana
- 1–2 tsp. banana extract
- 1/2 cup strawberries
- 1/4 cup soy milk
- 6 oz. of nonfat or one percent milk
- 9 1/2 oz. (1/2 cake) silken tofu artificial sweetener to taste

ing foods like rice and bananas. But what if our naturally occurring melatonin levels are too high? What if we sleep too much or can't wake up in the morning? Melatonin production drops when the sun rises. Using bright lights to imitate the sun can trick our bodies into thinking it's daytime and help us feel more alert.

Bright Light Therapy

Before we had the lightbulb, people went to bed when the sun went down and got up when the sun came up. Our sleep patterns and biological clocks were based on light and darkness. Thomas Edison's illuminating invention ruined all that by making light a twenty-four hour possibility!

As we noted earlier, in daylight our melatonin levels go down, which triggers the brain to become more active for our waking hours. If this process were described in a formula it might look like this:

Light › low melatonin = wake-up time
Dark › high melatonin = time to sleep

lux: A unit of measure of light brightness.

For people who have difficulty waking or feeling alert in the morning, using bright lights can depress their melatonin levels and jump-start their brains. This is especially true for people whose internal clocks are off (due to jet lag, overnight shift work, or delayed sleep phase) or for people who struggle with excessive winter sleepiness related to seasonal depression. Bright lights trick the brain into thinking that it's daylight.

To get the best result from bright light therapy, a person who has difficulty waking should expose themselves to sunlight or bright lights first thing in the morning. They should avoid bright light later in the day.

For the person who tends to fall asleep too early in the evening, who just can't stay awake long enough at night to enable them to sleep through until morning, the exact opposite is true: They should

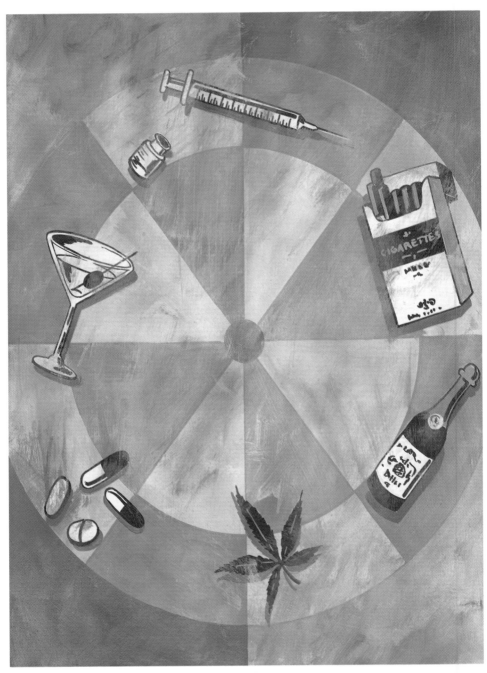

Drugs, nicotine, and alcohol can all interfere with our bodies' natural clocks.

put themselves in front of a light box during the late evening hours to delay their onset of sleep.

A light box is a specially designed, high-intensity white light made specifically for light therapy uses. Recommended brightness for this kind of light is about twenty times brighter than your average household lamp, or ten thousand lux. On average, light boxes cost between $200 and $500 (U.S.), but are well worth the investment if you struggle with morning fatigue. They are not only useful for combating sleep disorders but depression as well.

Most doctors and sleep specialists recommend the following:

- Sit within fifteen to twenty inches of the light.
- Stay in front of the light for fifteen minutes to two hours.
- For those having trouble getting up in the morning, schedule your time in front of the light as close to waking as possible, usually between six and eight a.m.
- For those having difficulty staying awake long enough into the evening, schedule your light time for around eight p.m.
- Make sure your light has a UV (ultraviolet) filter to protect you against harmful rays or take necessary precautions (as you would if your were in the sun).

Doctors often prescribe bright light therapy in conjunction with another alternate sleep treatment: chronotherapy.

Chronotherapy

Remember Carrie from chapter five who couldn't get to sleep before three or four o'clock in the morning? Do you recall how she couldn't "back up" on the "one-way street" that represented her internal biological clock? To get to an earlier bedtime, Carrie had to fast-forward all the way around the clock to a better bedtime. Carrie's drive around the block used a process called chronotherapy.

Carrie delayed her bedtime by an hour each night for nearly two weeks. That meant that for a few days over those two weeks, Carrie went to sleep in the afternoon or early evening and had to wake up eight hours later while it was still dark. Bright light therapy could have helped her body think it was daytime when it was really night.

For a person who wants a normal bedtime whose delayed internal clock causes her not to fall asleep until 4:00 a.m., a chronotherapy schedule that includes light box therapy might look something like this:

Night #1: Go to sleep at 4:00 a.m., wake at noon.
Night #2: Go to sleep at 6:00 a.m., wake at 2:00 p.m.
Night #3: Go to sleep at 8:00 a.m., wake at 4:00 p.m.
Night #4: Go to sleep at 10:00 a.m., wake at 6:00 p.m.
Night #5: Go to sleep at noon, wake at 8:00 p.m. (use light box)
Night #6: Go to sleep at 2:00 p.m., wake at 10:00 p.m. (use light box)
Night #7: Go to sleep at 4:00 p.m., wake at midnight (use light box)
Night #8: Go to sleep at 6:00 p.m., wake at 2:00 a.m. (use light box)
Night #9: Go to sleep at 8:00 p.m., wake at 4:00 a.m. (use light box)
Night #10: Go to sleep at 10:00 p.m., wake at 6:00 a.m. (use light box)

By progressively changing her sleep time and by using a light box to help her body adjust to different waking times, this person was able to get her internal clock to synchronize with a normal sleep/wake schedule in just ten days. Chronotherapy combined with bright light therapy worked for her.

For people like sleep-delayed Carrie, restless-legged Kevin, and others, drugs are not the first or best choice for treating their sleep disorders. These patients often find help in herbs, vitamins, minerals, and other dietary supplements. Even hormone augmentation using products like melatonin can induce sleep. And for those who don't want to take any substances at all, chronotherapy and bright light therapy can provide the help they need.

We take sleep for granted—until our sleep patterns are interrupted. Then sleep becomes a precious commodity.

Dietary supplements and lifestyle changes can help people to synchronize their internal clocks with the natural patterns of day and night.

When you combine these alternatives with good sleep habits and a healthy lifestyle, medications may not be needed at all. But for some people, sleep disorder drugs are an essential part of their treatment plan. In either case, most people with sleep disorders can be treated successfully today.

Further Reading

Bayer, Linda. *Sleep Disorders*. Philadelphia: Chelsea House, 2001.

Drummond, Dr. Edward. *The Complete Guide to Psychiatric Drugs: Straight Talk for Best Results*. New York: John Wiley and Sons, 2006.

Erichsen, Daniel. *Sleep 101*. Boca Raton, Fla.: Universal Publishers, 2012.

Foldvary-Schaefer, Nancy. *The Cleveland Clinic Guide to Sleep Disorders*. New York: Kaplan Publishing, 2009.

Schenck, Carlos H. *Sleep: A Groundbreaking Guide to the Mysteries, the Problems, and the Solutions*. New York: Penguin, 2007.

Wilens, Dr. Timothy. *Straight Talk about Psychiatric Medications for Kids*. New York: The Guilford Press, 2008.

For More Information

American Academy of Child and Adolescent Psychiatry
www.aacap.org

American Academy of Sleep Medicine (AASM)
www.aasmnet.org

American Psychiatric Association
www.psych.org

American Sleep Apnea Association
www.sleepapnea.org

Canadian Mental Health Association
www.cmha.ca

Substance Abuse and Mental Health services Administration
www.samhsa.gov

Narcolepsy Network
www.narcolepsynetwork.org

National Institute of Mental Health
www.nimh.nih.gov

National Mental Health Association
www.nmha.org

National Sleep Foundation
www.sleepfoundation.org

Restless Leg Syndrome (RLS)
www.rls.org

Publisher's Note:
The websites listed on this page were active at the time of publication. The publisher is not responsible for websites that have changed their address or discontinued operation since the date of publication. The publisher will review and update the websites upon each reprint.

Index

About the Author & Consultants

Joan Esherick is a full-time author, freelance writer, and professional speaker who lives outside of Philadelphia, Pennsylvania. Joan has contributed dozens of articles to national print periodicals, written spiritual and educational books, and speaks nationwide.

Mary Ann McDonnell, Ph.D., R.N., is the owner of South Shore Psychiatric Services, where she provides psychiatric services to children and adolescents. She has worked as a psychiatric nurse at Franciscan Hospital for Children and has been a clinical instructor for Northeastern University and Boston College advanced-practice nursing students. She was also the director of clinical trials in the pediatric psychopharmacology research unit at Massachusetts General Hospital. Her areas of expertise are bipolar disorder in children and adolescents, ADHD, and depression.

Donald Esherick has worked in regulatory affairs at Rhone-Poulenc Rorer, Wyeth Pharmaceuticals, Pfizer, and Pharmalink Consulting. He specializes in the chemistry section (manufacture and testing) of investigational and marketed drugs.